Tell me another
JOKE

Tell me another
JOKE

Tell me another JOKE

Compiled by RALPH UNDERWOOD

Pictures by SUSAN PERL

GROSSET & DUNLAP · Publishers · NEW YORK

There were three dry-cleaning stores on one block in a big city, and the competition for business was quite fierce. At last, one of the stores put up a big sign in the window:

BEST DRY-CLEANERS
IN THE CITY

About a week later, the second store blossomed forth with a bigger sign:

BEST DRY-CLEANERS
IN THE WORLD

And a week after that, the third store put up a modest little sign:

BEST DRY-CLEANERS
ON THE BLOCK

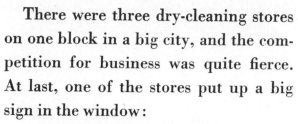

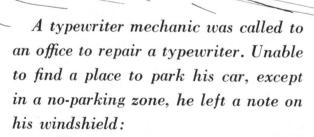

A typewriter mechanic was called to an office to repair a typewriter. Unable to find a place to park his car, except in a no-parking zone, he left a note on his windshield:

"Sid Karp, typewriter mechanic, working inside of building."

When he returned to his car, he found a ticket on the windshield, and another note:

"John MacDonald, police officer, working outside of building."

WIFE: "I'm going to give you a piece of my mind!"
HUSBAND: "Darling, do you think you can spare it?"

A little boy got a small boomerang for his birthday. He enjoyed it as he had never enjoyed anything in his life. All day long he would throw out his boomerang and catch it as it returned to him.

His parents decided to buy him a larger, shinier boomerang for his next birthday, but when he got it, the poor lad cracked up.

He went crazy trying to throw the old boomerang away!

When you tell a joke to a hyena, he
  laughs three times.
First, when you tell it.
Then when you explain it to him.
And finally, when he understands it.
When you tell a joke to a Dodo, he
  laughs twice.
First, when you tell it.
Then when you explain it to him.
He never understands it.
When you tell a joke to a donkey, he
  laughs once.
When you tell it to him.
He doesn't want it explained.
And he wouldn't understand it anyway.
When you tell a joke to an owl, he
  never laughs.
Before you are finished he always says,
"Who! I heard that years ago."

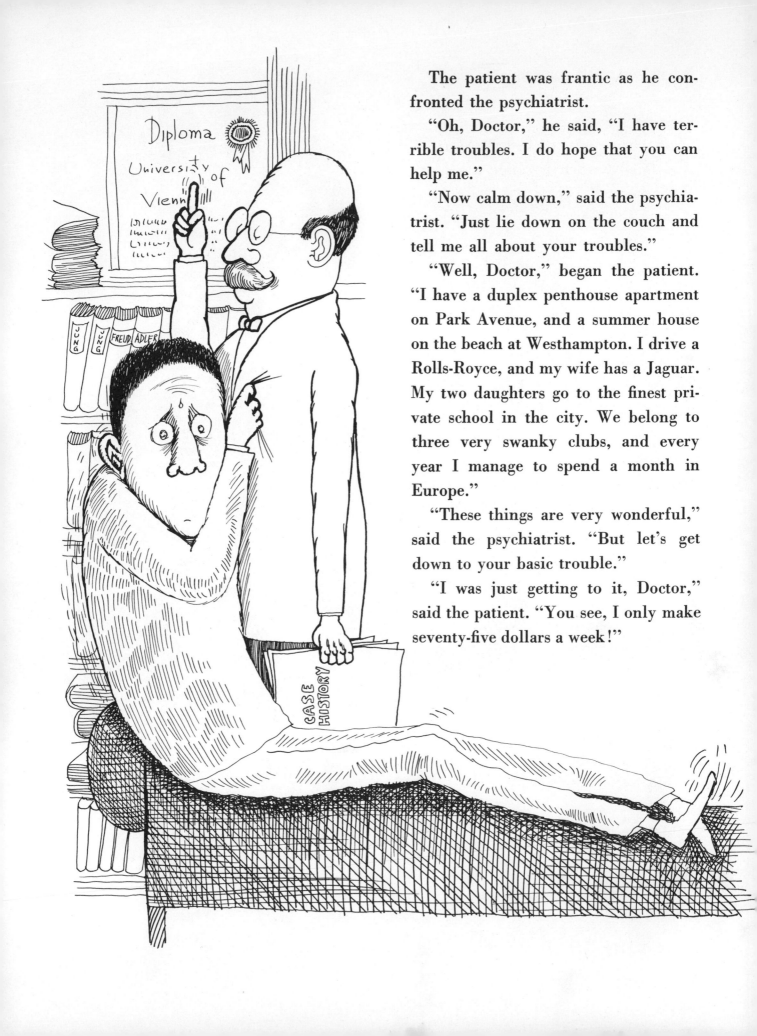

The patient was frantic as he confronted the psychiatrist.

"Oh, Doctor," he said, "I have terrible troubles. I do hope that you can help me."

"Now calm down," said the psychiatrist. "Just lie down on the couch and tell me all about your troubles."

"Well, Doctor," began the patient. "I have a duplex penthouse apartment on Park Avenue, and a summer house on the beach at Westhampton. I drive a Rolls-Royce, and my wife has a Jaguar. My two daughters go to the finest private school in the city. We belong to three very swanky clubs, and every year I manage to spend a month in Europe."

"These things are very wonderful," said the psychiatrist. "But let's get down to your basic trouble."

"I was just getting to it, Doctor," said the patient. "You see, I only make seventy-five dollars a week!"

Matthew, Mark, Luke, and John
Stole a cow, and away they run.
The cow got loose, they stole a goose,
And they all got thrown in the
    calaboose.

Matthew, Mark, Luke and John
Stole a cart, and away they run.
The cart got broke, they stole a pail,
and they all wound up in the county
    jail.

MOTHER: "If you were a good father, you would take Junior to the zoo."
FATHER: "I will not. If the zoo wants him, let them come and get him!"

A man went to see his doctor. He was suffering from acute anxiety and seemed on the verge of a nervous breakdown. After the examination the doctor went into the consultation room to discuss the case with the patient's wife.

"What your husband needs most of all is rest and quiet," said the doctor. "Here are some tranquilizer pills. You should take one every three hours!"

One hot Sunday in church, the minister was in the middle of a long sermon when Mr. Jones fell asleep. This was bad enough, but in a short while Mr. Jones began to snore very loudly.

Interrupting his sermon, the minister leaned forward and said:

"Tommy Jones, will you kindly wake up your father?"

Replied Tommy, "Wake him yourself, Reverend. You put him to sleep!"

A man was on his way to an airport, and he stopped at a drugstore. There was a fortune-telling scale near the door, and since the man was curious as to how much excess baggage he would be charged for, he placed his suitcase on the scale and put in a penny.

The card that came out read as follows:

"You weigh forty-eight pounds.

"You are too good-natured and let other people take advantage of you. Be more firm in the future!"

MRS. SMITH: *"Doctor, I wish you would speak to my husband about his smoking."*

DOCTOR: *"But, Mrs. Smith, many men smoke!"*

MRS. SMITH: *"I know, Doctor, but he inhales."*

DOCTOR: *"Lots of smokers inhale!"*

MRS. SMITH: *"But, Doctor, he doesn't exhale!"*

SID: "My wife is always bothering me for money."

BARNEY: "What does she do with it?"

SID: "How should I know? I never give her any."

Several fishermen were fishing off the same bridge. One man observed the man next to him hook a large bass, reel it in, and then throw it back into the lake. A while later, the same fisherman landed a giant pike, took it off the hook, and again threw it back. Finally, the fisherman caught a small perch. This fish he put into his creel, and then he proceeded to pack up his fishing gear.

"Pardon me," said the man who had observed this, "but I am curious as to why you threw back those two large fish and then kept this small one."

"I have a small frying pan!" answered the fisherman.

Mr. Dash had just finished a wonderful meal in a restaurant. The waiter brought over the check, and Mr. Dash fumbled around in his pockets, looking for money.

"That's strange," he said. "I seem to have left my money at home. I'm afraid you'll have to let me owe it to you."

"Oh, it's perfectly all right," said the waiter. "I'll just write your name on the wall over here, and the amount of money that you owe."

"Oh, don't do that!" said Mr. Dash. "Everyone will see it!"

"No, they won't," said the waiter, "because your overcoat will be hanging right over it."

A rabbi and a priest were great friends and always teasing each other. One night, at a banquet, the main course was ham, and the rabbi, of course, couldn't partake of it because of his religious customs.

"When are you going to weaken, Rabbi," said the priest, "and finally take a taste of pork?"

"At your wedding, Father!" answered the rabbi.

Mr. Beer had a serious operation and he went to Florida to recuperate. However, instead of getting better, he got worse, and at the end of two months he died. The body was shipped home for burial. At the funeral parlor one of his friends was viewing the body and said to the widow:

"Doesn't he look nice in the coffin!"

"Of course," said the widow. "Those two months in Florida did him a world of good!"

The little girl had just returned from Sunday school, and was having dinner with her family. She asked her father when her baby brother would be able to talk.

"Oh, he won't talk until he's about two years old," said her father.

"That's too bad," said the little girl. "It was much better in the olden days when babies could talk right away."

"What makes you say that. babies could talk right away in the olden days?" asked her father.

"Why, we read it in the Bible in Sunday school," said the little girl. "We were reading the Book of Job, and it said 'Job cursed the day he was born'!"

Many people have trouble understanding the customs of others which may seem strange to them — although their own are just as strange. So an American who had come to put flowers on a friend's grave, was amused to see a Chinese gentleman coming to put food and drink on his friend's grave — as is the custom in China.

"Say," asked the American rudely, "when do you expect your friend to come out and eat that food?"

The Chinese man bowed politely and said, "The same time that your esteemed friend comes out to smell the flowers."

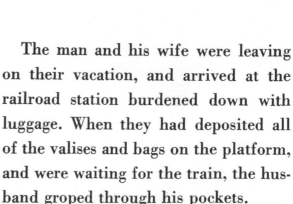

The man and his wife were leaving on their vacation, and arrived at the railroad station burdened down with luggage. When they had deposited all of the valises and bags on the platform, and were waiting for the train, the husband groped through his pockets.

"Gosh, dear," said the husband, "I wish I had thought to bring along the piano."

"The piano?" asked the wife. "What on earth would we need that for?"

"Our railroad tickets are on it."

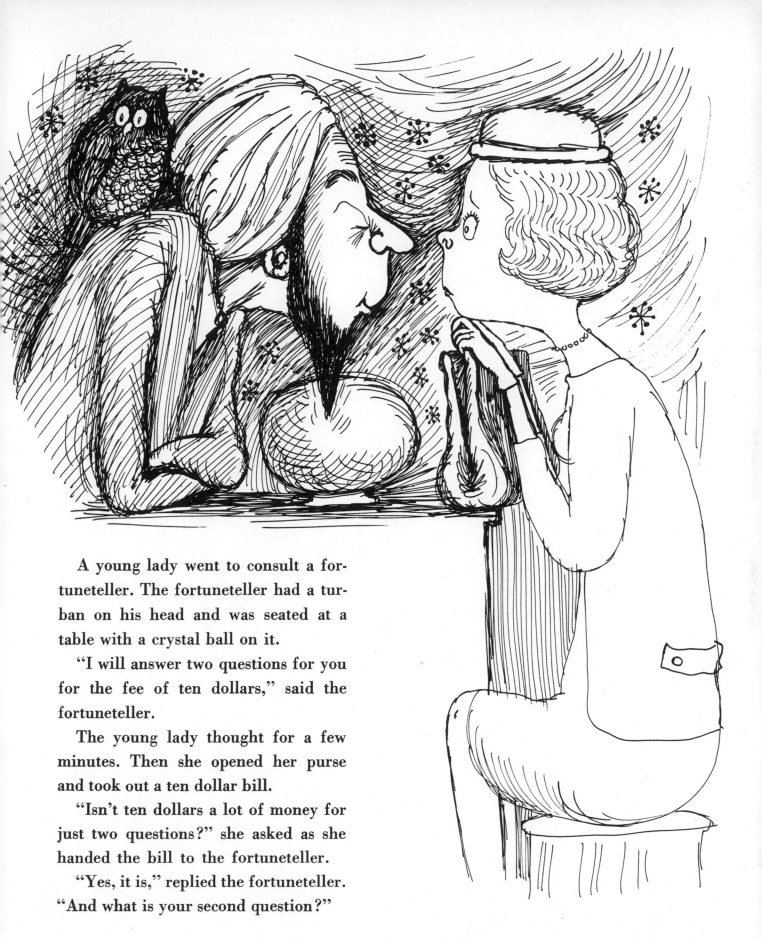

A young lady went to consult a fortuneteller. The fortuneteller had a turban on his head and was seated at a table with a crystal ball on it.

"I will answer two questions for you for the fee of ten dollars," said the fortuneteller.

The young lady thought for a few minutes. Then she opened her purse and took out a ten dollar bill.

"Isn't ten dollars a lot of money for just two questions?" she asked as she handed the bill to the fortuneteller.

"Yes, it is," replied the fortuneteller. "And what is your second question?"

JUDGE: "Are you the defendant in this case?"

SIMPLE SAM: "No, your Honor. I'm the fellow who stole the car."

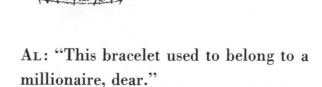

AL: "This bracelet used to belong to a millionaire, dear."

SAL: "Really, darling? Who?"

AL: "Woolworth!"

BROWN: "Did you speak to your wife about saving money?"

SMITH: "I certainly did!"

BROWN: "What was decided?"

SMITH: "I have to give up smoking."

CUSTOMER: "I'd like to buy a tombstone for my wife's grave."

SALESMAN: "But, sir, didn't I sell you a tombstone for your wife's grave about five years ago?"

CUSTOMER: "Yes, but I remarried."

SALESMAN: "Oh, congratulations!"

SAM: "My wife got a terrific new mud-pack treatment at the beauty parlor last week!"
BUD: "Did it work well?"
SAM: "She was gorgeous for three days — then the mud fell off."

BRIDE: "Darling, I have a confession to make. I don't know how to cook."
GROOM: "Honey, I have a confession to make, too. I have no job — so it won't matter very much."

MRS. CHIPS: "Your husband seems to be a man of rare gifts."
MRS. CHOPS: "Oh, he is! The last one he gave me was fifteen years ago."

TEACHER: "What can you tell me about the Chinese people?"
STUDENT: "They are stupid!"
TEACHER: "What makes you say that?"
STUDENT: "It says in the book that the population of China is the densest in the world!"

One day part of the wall between Heaven and Hell broke down and Saint Peter called up the Devil and asked him to fix it.

"The break definitely came from your side," said Peter, "and it's up to you to make the necessary repairs."

"I'm sorry," said the Devil, "but I don't care about fixing it. If you want it done, do it yourself."

"In that case," said Peter, "I'm afraid I'll have to sue you."

"Ha! Ha!" laughed the Devil. "And where would you find a lawyer?"

Letter from camp: "Dear folks, please send food packages. All they serve here is breakfast, lunch, and dinner."

A man suffered from the delusion that he was a dog, so he went to a psychiatrist for treatment. After a year of psychiatric treatment, he met a friend who had heard of his trouble.

"How are you feeling?" asked the friend.

"Fine," replied the man. "Just feel my nose!"

The motorcycle policeman waved the motorist over to the side of the road. When they had both stopped, the officer walked over to the car and said very angrily:

"How come you didn't stop back there when I blew my whistle, and later when I went after you and sounded my siren?"

"I'm sorry, officer," said the motorist, "but I didn't hear you. I must be getting hard of hearing."

"Well, don't worry about that," said the officer sarcastically. "You'll be getting your hearing — in court, tomorrow morning!"

The Bishop was dying. The doctor had left strict orders that no visitors were to be permitted unless their names were especially mentioned by the Bishop. Hundreds of high churchmen were turned away from the sickroom, and many notables of public life, but one man was admitted when he called. This man was a person of bad reputation, a non-believer, although he was a writer of some note and had been a friend of the Bishop.

After their conversation, the writer wondered aloud why he had been privileged to visit the Bishop while many, more worthy, had not.

"I feel certain that I will see my other friends in the next world," said the Bishop. "This is probably the last time I will have to see you!"

"That new throughway has ruined my motel business," complained Ezra.

"Why, Ezra," said Zeke, "how can you say that? Every night when I pass your place on my way home, I see a 'No Vacancy' sign."

"That's so," admitted Ezra, "but I used to have to turn away fifty people every night. Now I only have to turn away ten!"

A man came into a hotel lobby and went to the desk. It was quite late and he was very tired.

"I'd like a room for the night," he said to the clerk.

"I'm sorry, sir," said the desk clerk, "but the hotel is full. I'm afraid there are no rooms available."

"Oh, I'm sure that you always have one or two rooms that you keep in reserve for emergencies," said the man. "If the President of the United States came in tonight, wouldn't you be able to arrange a room for him?"

"Oh, yes," said the clerk. "We can always provide accommodations for the President."

"Well," said the man, "I happen to know that he won't be here tonight, so you can just give me his room."

Mr. Russell, the Texas oilman, drove up to the airport in his Rolls-Royce limousine. The chauffeur helped him out and then drove away. Mr. Russell carried his own bag to the airline desk.

"Son," he said to the clerk, "my name is Russell and I want a ticket on the next plane to Honolulu."

"I'm sorry, Mr. Russell," said the clerk, "but our flights to Honolulu are filled for the next two weeks."

"Son," said Mr. Russell as he took his wallet out of his pocket, "you look like a very efficient boy to me. I wouldn't be surprised to find you the president of this airline in a few years."

Then Mr. Russell pulled a nice, new, crisp, one hundred dollar bill out of his wallet and laid it on the counter.

"I'm going to the coffee shop for a cup of coffee," said Mr. Russell. "You see what you can arrange while I'm gone."

Ten minutes later, Mr. Russell strolled back to the airlines counter.

"Oh, Mr. Russell," said the clerk excitedly. "We had a cancellation at the last minute, and I've put your bag on the plane. Please hurry — the plane is being held up for you."

"Thank you, son," said Mr. Russell as he headed for the gate.

Ten hours later the plane landed at the airport in Honolulu. Mr. Russell took a taxi to the best hotel, went to the desk, and summoned the clerk.

"Son," he said, "my name is Russell and I hear you have a Presidential suite in this hotel that is really the last word. I'd like to rent it for the next two weeks."

"I'm sorry, sir," answered the clerk, "but the entire hotel is booked for the next month, and the Presidential suite is reserved for the next year."

"Son," said Mr. Russell, as he took his wallet out of his pocket, "you look like a very efficient boy to me. I wouldn't be surprised to find you the manager of this hotel in a few years."

Then Mr. Russell pulled a nice, new, crisp, one hundred dollar bill out of his wallet and laid it on the counter.

"I'm going to the coffee shop for a cup of coffee," said Mr. Russell. "You see what you can arrange while I'm gone."

Ten minutes later, Mr. Russell strolled back to the hotel desk.

"Oh, Mr. Russell," said the clerk excitedly, "the people in the Presidential suite had a sudden change of plans, and you can have it for the next two weeks. Please follow the bellhop who has your bag, and he will take you to your suite."

"Thank you, son," said Mr. Russell as he headed for the elevator.

A half-hour later, Mr. Russell came out on the beach. He called over the beach boy.

"Son," he said, "my name is Russell, and I'd like a cabana and a private

stretch of beach for the next two weeks."

"I'm sorry, sir," said the beach boy, "but all of our cabanas are rented for the next month, and as for a private beach, that would be impossible."

"Son," said Mr. Russell, taking his wallet out of his robe, "I'm going back to my room to change my swimming trunks."

He pulled a nice, new, crisp, one hundred dollar bill out of the wallet and pressed it into the beach boy's hand.

"You see what you can arrange while I'm gone," he said.

Ten minutes later, as Mr. Russell strolled back onto the beach, he found a private cabana waiting for him, with a nice private stretch of beach roped off with a velvet rope.

"Is everything all right?" asked the beach boy solicitously, as Mr. Russell settled himself on the chaise lounge.

"Fine, son, just fine!" said Mr. Russell.

"You know, son," he added, "when I relax on these golden sands, and look out at the green ocean, and up at the blue sky and feel the warm sun and the soft breezes on my skin, I realize that these are the true and important things in life.

"When I get in a spot like this, I always say to myself, 'Russell, the best things in life are free. Russell, who needs money?' "

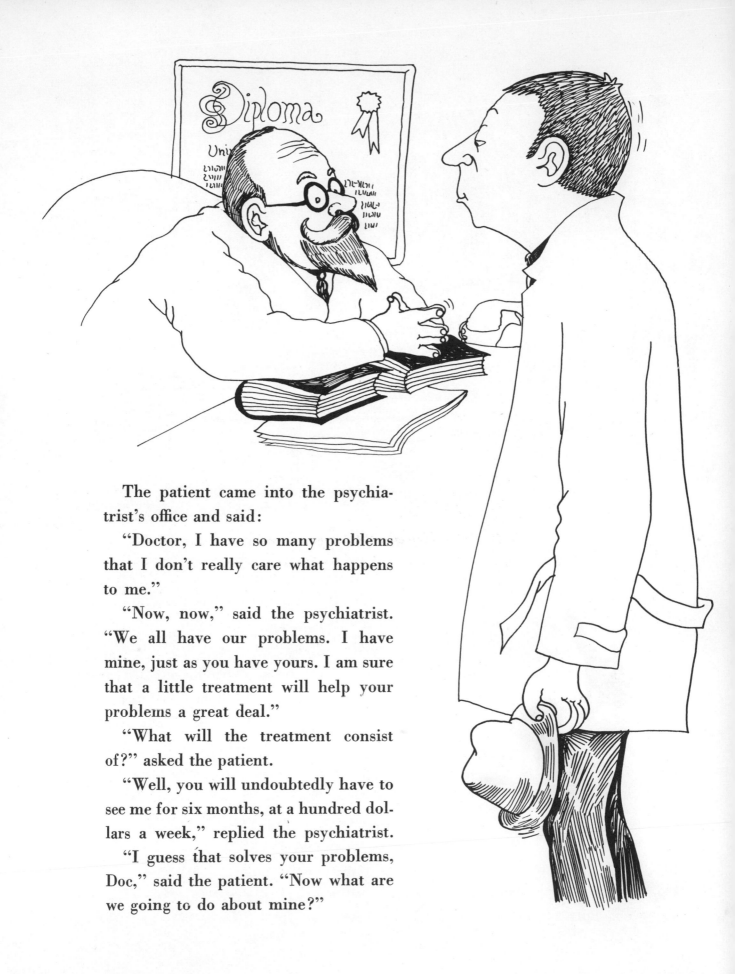

The patient came into the psychiatrist's office and said:

"Doctor, I have so many problems that I don't really care what happens to me."

"Now, now," said the psychiatrist. "We all have our problems. I have mine, just as you have yours. I am sure that a little treatment will help your problems a great deal."

"What will the treatment consist of?" asked the patient.

"Well, you will undoubtedly have to see me for six months, at a hundred dollars a week," replied the psychiatrist.

"I guess that solves your problems, Doc," said the patient. "Now what are we going to do about mine?"

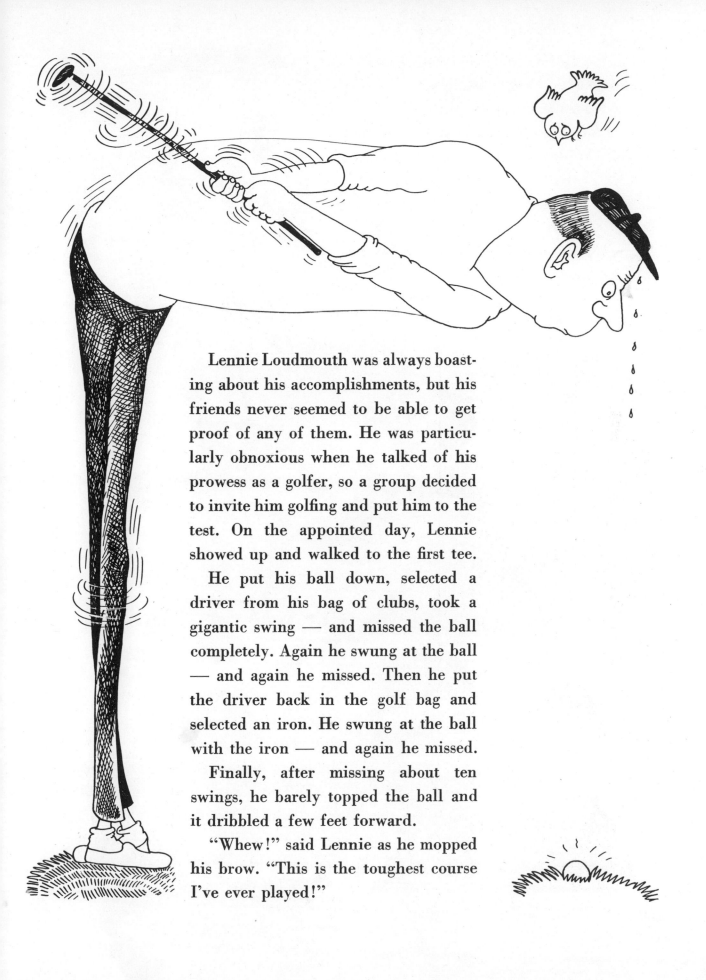

Lennie Loudmouth was always boasting about his accomplishments, but his friends never seemed to be able to get proof of any of them. He was particularly obnoxious when he talked of his prowess as a golfer, so a group decided to invite him golfing and put him to the test. On the appointed day, Lennie showed up and walked to the first tee.

He put his ball down, selected a driver from his bag of clubs, took a gigantic swing — and missed the ball completely. Again he swung at the ball — and again he missed. Then he put the driver back in the golf bag and selected an iron. He swung at the ball with the iron — and again he missed.

Finally, after missing about ten swings, he barely topped the ball and it dribbled a few feet forward.

"Whew!" said Lennie as he mopped his brow. "This is the toughest course I've ever played!"

A painter came over to a ladder upon which his assistant was standing and painting the ceiling.

"Say, John," he asked, "are you holding on tight to that brush?"

"I sure am," replied John. "Why do you ask?"

"Well, if you are," said the painter, "you won't mind if I borrow this ladder for a few minutes!"

Two psychiatrists were leaving their respective offices at the end of the day. One looked worn and bedraggled, while the other one looked fresh and chipper.

"Tell me," asked the tired-looking one, "how can you listen to the heart-rending complaints of your patients all day and still manage to look so well?"

"Who listens?" was the response.

An actor had achieved fame portraying Abraham Lincoln on the stage, and afterwards he began to pattern his own appearance offstage after the Great Emancipator.

One day, as he was walking down Broadway with his stovepipe hat and black cape, another actor looked after him and said:

"That fellow won't be really happy until he's assassinated!"

KNOCK, KNOCK

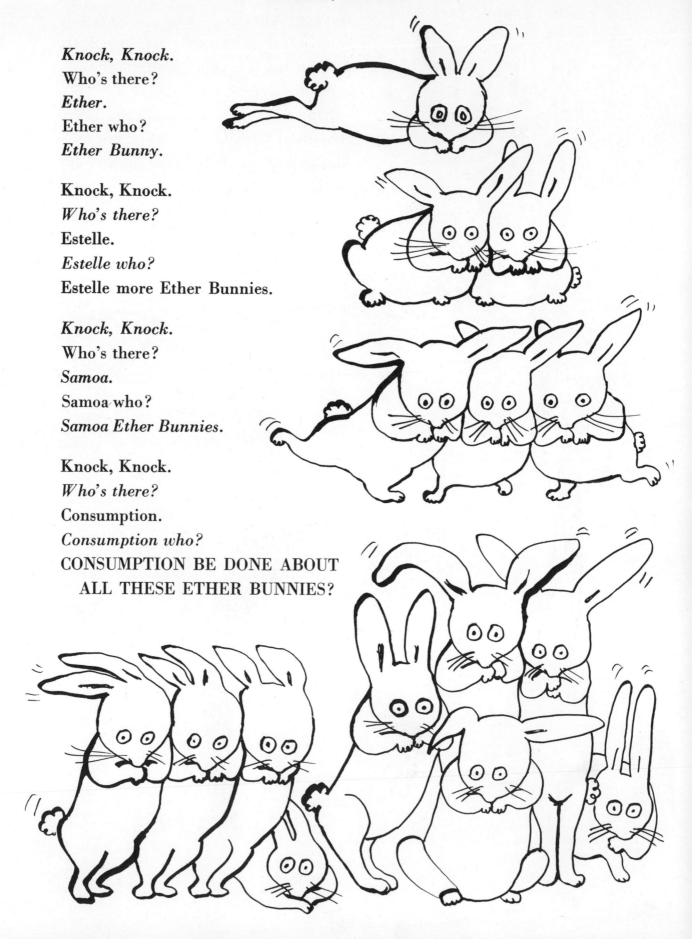

Knock, Knock.
Who's there?
Ether.
Ether who?
Ether Bunny.

Knock, Knock.
Who's there?
Estelle.
Estelle who?
Estelle more Ether Bunnies.

Knock, Knock.
Who's there?
Samoa.
Samoa who?
Samoa Ether Bunnies.

Knock, Knock.
Who's there?
Consumption.
Consumption who?
CONSUMPTION BE DONE ABOUT
ALL THESE ETHER BUNNIES?

Knock, Knock.
Who's there?
Banana.
Banana Who?
Banana, Banana.

Knock, Knock.
Who's there?
Banana.
Banana Who?
Banana, Banana.

Knock, Knock.
Who's there?
Banana.
BANANA WHO?
Banana, Banana.

Knock, Knock.
Who's there?
Orange.
ORANGE WHO?
Orange you glad I'm not a banana?

That's too bad.
What's too bad?
Life.
What's Life?
A magazine.
Where can I buy it?
All over.
How much?
Twenty-five cents.
But I only have a dime.
That's too bad.
What's too bad?
Life.
What's Life?
A magazine.
Where can I buy it?
All over.
How much?
Twenty-five cents.
But I only have a dime.
That's too bad.

The little girl in the first grade drew a picture of a cowboy walking through the swinging doors of a saloon. When the teacher gently implied that this was not a good subject for a picture, the little girl said:

"Oh, he's not going in there to drink whiskey, teacher. He's going in there to shoot a man!"

Johnny was looking through the family photograph album.

"Say, Mom," he asked, "who's this curly-haired guy in this picture?"

His mother looked.

"That's your father, Johnny," she said.

Johnny looked puzzled for a few moments. Then he asked:

"Then who's that bald-headed guy upstairs?"

The patient sat down in the psychiatrist's office. The psychiatrist observed him closely.

"Now, just what seems to be your problem?" asked the psychiatrist.

"I keep eating strawberries," said the patient.

"Why, that doesn't sound so bad," said the psychiatrist. "I'm very fond of strawberries, myself, and I eat them every chance I get."

"Off the wallpaper?" asked the patient.

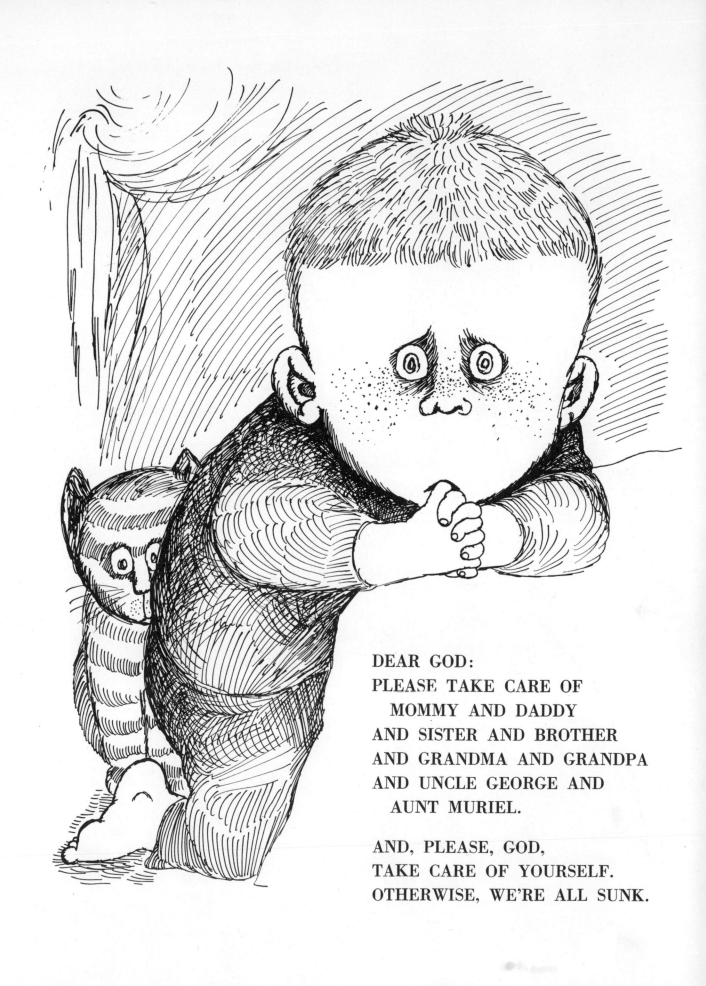

DEAR GOD:
PLEASE TAKE CARE OF
 MOMMY AND DADDY
AND SISTER AND BROTHER
AND GRANDMA AND GRANDPA
AND UNCLE GEORGE AND
 AUNT MURIEL.

AND, PLEASE, GOD,
TAKE CARE OF YOURSELF.
OTHERWISE, WE'RE ALL SUNK.

Way down south where the cotton grows,
A mouse stepped on an elephant's toes.
Said the elephant with tears in his eyes,
"Why don't you pick on someone your
    size?"
"Don't throw your weight at me, you
    pill!"
Said the mouse. "Can't you see I've
    been ill?"

Sherlock Holmes, the great detective, was sitting in his study smoking his pipe and reading a book. There was a knock on the door, and his trusty friend and assistant, Dr. Watson, entered.

"Good day, Watson," said the great detective. "Don't you think it is a bit warm to be wearing your red flannel underwear?"

"What a magnificent bit of detection and deduction, Holmes!" exclaimed Watson. "But how on earth did you figure out that I am still wearing my red flannel underwear?"

"Elementary, my dear Watson," said Holmes. "You've neglected to put your trousers on!"

Woman on telephone: "Hello, Missing Persons Bureau? I'd like to make a report. My husband disappeared six days ago, and I haven't heard a word from him."

Officer: "Yes, ma'am. If you will kindly give me a complete description of your husband, we will put it on the teletype and send out a seven-state alarm at once."

Woman: "Well, he's very short, quite fat, and bowlegged. He's completely bald and he dresses very sloppily. He has false teeth that don't fit very well . . . Officer, perhaps I'd better forget the whole thing, and not bother with the missing person alarm at all."

SON: "Dad, what's an ocelot?"

FATHER: "It's Sir Ocelot, son, and he was one of King Arthur's Knights of the Round Table."

SON: "Dad, what's algebra?"

FATHER: "It's the language the people speak in Algeria, son."

SON: "Dad, what do they call people who live in Paris, France?"

FATHER: "Parasites, son."

SON: "Dad, you don't mind me asking you all these questions, do you?"

FATHER: "Of course not, son. How else can you ever become educated?"

Poor Dad was trying to enjoy a quiet day of rest at home.

At the breakfast table Jane asked him, "Dad, will you drive me over to Jill's house?"

So he took the car out of the garage and drove her the five blocks to her friend's house. No sooner had he returned, when Tom asked him, "Dad, will you drive Bill and me to the swimming pool?"

So Dad drove them to the swimming pool, which was six blocks away.

That afternoon, after he had picked up both children, he became a bit indignant.

"I don't know what's the matter with children today," he said. "You kids have to be driven everyplace, even if it is only a few blocks away. Don't you know what feet are for?"

"Of course," they both answered. "The left one is for the brake, and the right one is for the gas!"

Delivery Man: "Ma'am, this package is marked C.O.D."

Housewife: "Sounds fishy to me."

Dear Dad,

Thing$ are pretty good here at $chool, but they could be better. $ome thing$ are needed mo$t de$perately. I hope that you can gue$$ what I mean, and $end $ome $oon.

Your loving $on.

Dear Son,

NOthing is new here. I kNOw that you are doing better NOw than you have been. Write aNOther letter soon. I want to get this off in the NOon mail, so I'll sign off NOw.

Love, Dad.

Joe: "My doctor told me that I must give up smoking and drinking."
Moe: "What are you going to do?"
Joe: "Get a new doctor."

PATIENT: "Doctor, how much will my upper bridge cost?"
DENTIST: "It will be one hundred dollars."
PATIENT: "Couldn't you do it for eighty dollars?"
DENTIST: "Oh, all right."
PATIENT: "And how much will the lower bridge be?"
DENTIST: "One hundred and fifty dollars."
PATIENT: "Could you please do it for one hundred twenty-five dollars?"
DENTIST: "Well, all right, I'll make a special fee in your case."
PATIENT: "And doctor, what time is my appointment for tomorrow?"
DENTIST: "Eleven o'clock."
PATIENT: "Doctor, could you please make it ten-thirty?"

There was once an airplane stunt pilot who had a friend who had never been up in an airplane in his life. Neither had the friend's wife. The pilot used to tease them about being afraid to fly, and they always claimed that they were not afraid. So, finally, to settle the argument, the pilot made a bet with the man that he couldn't go for a plane ride with his wife and stay up for a half hour without crying out in fear.

On the appointed day, the three of them went to the airport and climbed into the pilot's open cockpit plane. The pilot was in the front seat, and the man and his wife were in the back seat.

As soon as the plane had gained enough altitude, the pilot went into a terrifying series of maneuvers. He did a barrel roll, a crash dive, a loop-the-loop, an outside loop, and several other breath-taking stunts. There was no sound from the back cockpit.

Finally, after the half hour was over, and the pilot had landed the plane and taxied back to the hanger, he spoke into the microphone:

"Congratulations, friend!" he said. "I've got to hand it to you. For someone who has never flown before to go through a flight like that without crying out, takes real courage."

"Thank you," said his friend. "But you almost had me about halfway through — when my wife fell out!"

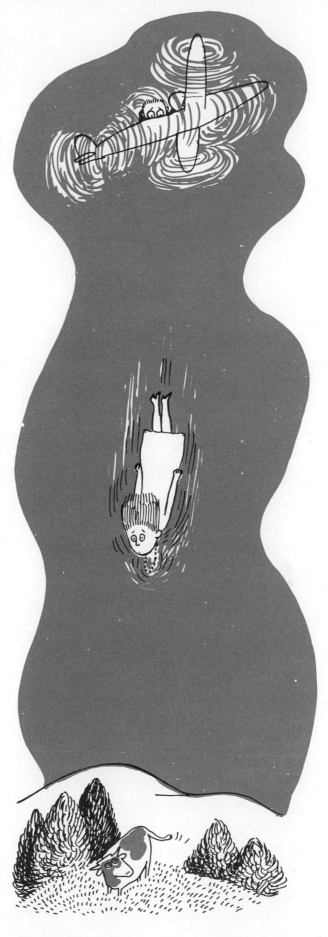

Mrs. A.: "What do you find is the best kind of dishwasher?"
Mrs. B.: "My husband."

Husband on phone: "Darling, I'm having an argument with Bill at the club. Is it all right if I tell him I'm not henpecked?"

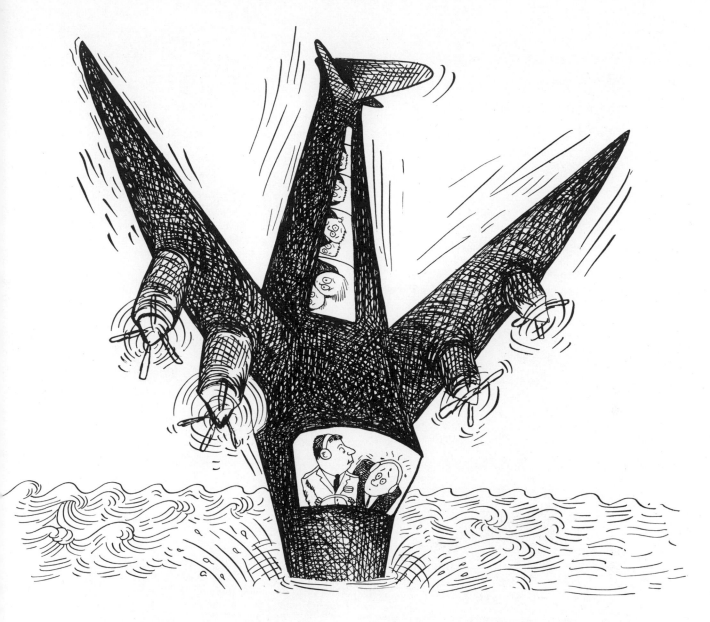

Captain Landy, the airline pilot, awoke late. His alarm clock had failed to go off. While he was trying to shave quickly, he cut himself. The toast for breakfast got burnt, and there was no more bread left.

He rushed out to his car and found a flat tire, so he had to take a taxicab to the airport. He got there late and got a bawling out from his boss.

Finally he took off in the giant jet plane and was heading for Europe. About five hundred miles out, over the ocean, one of the four engines failed. A few minutes later the second one stopped. Then the third. And the fourth.

As the plane slowly headed into a nosedive, Captain Landy turned to his copilot:

"Did you ever have one of those days when nothing seems to turn out right?"

The little boy wouldn't eat his cereal for breakfast. His mother coaxed, cajoled, begged, implored, threatened, and finally she said:

"All right, if you won't eat your cereal, God will be angry."

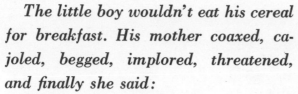

The little boy still refused to eat his cereal, and a few hours later a violent thunderstorm broke out. The sky grew black, the thunderclaps were like bombs falling, and the lightning flashed with an eerie glow.

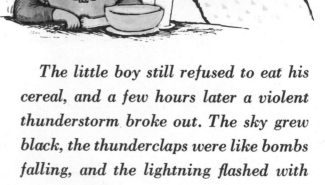

The little boy watched out the window, frightened. Then he said:

"I didn't think God would make such a fuss over a bowl of cereal!"

There's a hole in the middle of the sea.
There's a log in the hole in the middle
of the sea.
There's a bump on the log in the hole
in the middle of the sea.
There's a frog on the bump on the log
in the hole in the middle of the sea.
There's a fly on the frog on the bump
on the log in the hole in the middle
of the sea.
There's a wing on the fly on the frog
on the bump on the log in the hole
in the middle of the sea.
There's a flea on the wing of the fly on
the frog on the bump on the log in
the hole in the middle of the sea.
There's a head on the flea on the wing
of the fly on the frog on the bump
on the log in the hole in the middle
of the sea.
There's an eye in the head on the flea
on the wing of the fly on the frog on
the bump on the log in the hole in
the middle of the sea.
There's a gleam in the eye in the head
on the flea on the wing of the fly on
the frog on the bump on the log in
the hole in the middle of the sea.

Peter Piper worked on a farm.

His job was picking green peppers which were taken to a factory and pickled. So they were called pickled peppers.

When he picked them, he put them in a basket he carried on his arm. The basket was called a peck, because it held eight quarts of pickled peppers.

One day Peter Piper went out to pick pickled peppers.

There was a hole in the bottom of the peck.

All day Peter Piper picked pickled peppers, and all day they fell out of the hole in the bottom of the peck.

When Peter Piper came back from the fields, he went to the farmer.

"What work did you do, Peter Piper?" asked the farmer.

"I picked a peck of pickled peppers," said Peter Piper.

"Where are the pickled peppers, Peter Piper?" asked the farmer.

"Here in my peck," said Peter Piper.

But the peck was empty.

If Peter Piper picked a peck of pickled peppers, a peck of pickled peppers Peter Piper picked.

But if Peter Piper picked a peck of pickled peppers, where is the peck of pickled peppers that Peter Piper picked?

SHE: "Darling, I baked two kinds of cake today. Take your pick."

HE: "That probably won't be necessary, dear. My hammer and chisel should be sufficient."

I can't tell you the joke about the dirty window.

Why not?

You wouldn't see through it.

I can't tell you the joke about the roof.

Why not?

It's over your head.

I can't tell you the joke about the memory course.

Why not?

I forgot it.

But I will tell you the joke about the peacock.

How come?

It's a beautiful tale.

LIMERICKS

A fancy young dandy of Shoreham
Had pants made too tight, but he wore
  'em.
He looked very neat
Till he bent in the street
To pick up a dime — then he tore 'em.

There once was a dog named Saggy
Who was both tremendous and shaggy.
He was quite fierce and grim
On the front end of him,
But his back end was friendly and
    waggy.

The poor benighted Hindoo!
He does the best he kindoo.
He sticks to caste
From first to last.
For clothes, he makes his skindoo.

There was a young lady from Crete,
Who was so exceedingly neat,
When she got out of bed,
She stood on her head,
To keep from soiling her feet.

A rocket set out on a flight,
At a speed much faster than light.
It left one day
In a relative way,
And returned on the previous night.

A silly young lady named Stella,
Fell in love with a bow-legged fella.
When the loving chap
Let her sit on his lap,
She fell right through to the cella.

The teacher was conducting a class in American History, when she called on Johnny Smith.

"Johnny Smith, give me the name of one person who signed the Declaration of Independence," she said.

"I didn't do it, teacher," said Johnny.

"Just for that fresh remark, I want your mother to come and see me after school tomorrow," said the teacher.

The next afternoon, Mrs. Smith came to the classroom. Johnny had evidently told her of his problem.

She strode up to the teacher's desk and glared at her.

"Look, Mrs. Teacher!" she said. "My Johnny is a good, honest boy. Believe me, if he says he didn't do it, he didn't do it!"

A tramp was walking along the road when he chanced to pass a cemetery. Looking across the tombstones, he saw a lovely white marble mausoleum standing in the distance.

"Boy!" he said. "Those rich people sure know how to live!"

An indignant lady stalked up to the foreman of a big construction job and said:

"Sir, as I was passing by, my ears were assailed by the most blasphemous swearing and cursing I have ever heard in my life. If you do not immediately prevail upon your workmen to cease and desist, I shall have to make a complaint to the Police Department."

The foreman apologized to the lady and assured her that the matter would be properly attended to, and then he went to speak to the workmen.

"Now, boys," he said, "there has been a serious complaint that you have been using bad language, so that passers-by could hear it. Just what happened?"

"Oh, it was nothing," said Barney. "I was using the saw, and Pat was holding the wood, and the wood slipped, and the saw sliced off Pat's little finger — and Pat just said, 'Heavens to Betsy, Barney! I do wish that you would endeavor to be a bit more careful!' "

Hostess: "Oh, *do* have another of these caviar sandwiches!"

Guest: "Thank you, no. They're delicious, but I've already had three."

Hostess: "You've had seven, but who's counting?"

A rainy day was particularly difficult for the teacher at the nursery school. In the morning there were twenty raincoats and twenty pairs of rubbers and galoshes to be removed and put away. In the afternoon, the same garments had to be gotten out and put on again.

She was just finished struggling with the last pair of galoshes — it had been almost impossiblc to get them on — when the little boy looked up at her and said:

"Teacher, these aren't my galoshes."

"Oh, Heavens!" thought the teacher, as she wearily bent down and started to drag off the ill-fitting galoshes. "I wonder who went home with the wrong galoshes?"

"No," continued the little boy, as she struggled. "They're my brother's, and when they got too small for him, my mommy made me wear them!"

A visitor to the farm was asking all kinds of questions about the animals he saw.

"Why doesn't that cow have horns?" he inquired of the farmer.

"Well," drawled the farmer, "cows don't have horns for many reasons. Some have them removed, some kinds of cows never grow them, and some get them when they are old. That particular cow doesn't have them," he added, "because he's a horse!"

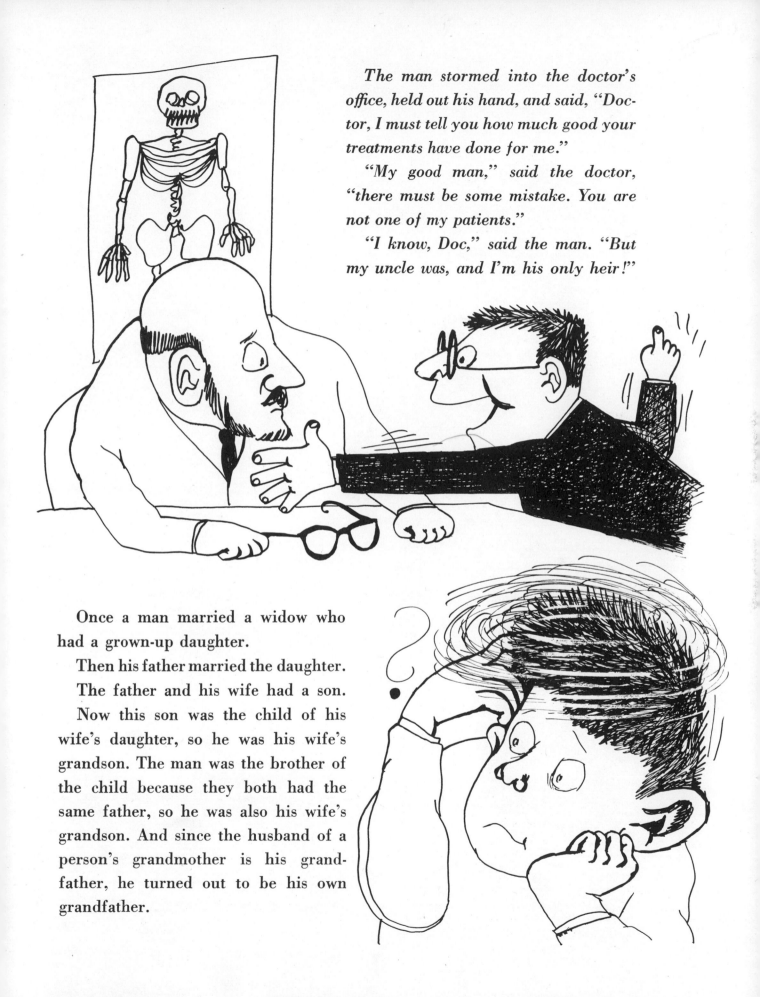

The man stormed into the doctor's office, held out his hand, and said, "Doctor, I must tell you how much good your treatments have done for me."

"My good man," said the doctor, "there must be some mistake. You are not one of my patients."

"I know, Doc," said the man. "But my uncle was, and I'm his only heir!"

Once a man married a widow who had a grown-up daughter.

Then his father married the daughter. The father and his wife had a son. Now this son was the child of his wife's daughter, so he was his wife's grandson. The man was the brother of the child because they both had the same father, so he was also his wife's grandson. And since the husband of a person's grandmother is his grandfather, he turned out to be his own grandfather.

A man and his wife made an agreement that the one who died first would try to contact the other one from the next world. The man passed away before his wife, and she was always on the alert for some manner of spirit message.

One evening as she sat in her living room she became aware of a ghostly presence.

"Darling! Is that you?" she asked.

"Yes," answered the ghostly presence.

"Tell me," she said, "how are things in the next world?"

"Just as lovely as can be," answered the ghostly presence. "Nothing but green rolling hills, a clear blue sky, fleecy white clouds, and clear pure air. And best of all, there is no work to do. All I do is romp and play the whole day through."

"How wonderful!" exclaimed the wife.

"Yes, it is," replied the ghostly presence. "And I have all the green grass to eat that I could ever desire."

"Grass?" asked the wife. "But you never used to like to eat grass!"

"I know," answered the ghostly presence. "But now I'm a bull in Montana!"

Sam had a big ugly scarecrow on the front lawn in front of his house. It was an eyesore in the neighborhood, and one day his next-door neighbor decided to complain.

"Say, Sam," said the neighbor, "that scarecrow is pretty ugly. Why on earth do you keep it in the front yard?"

"To scare the giraffes away," said Sam.

"That's silly!" said the neighbor. "I've never seen a giraffe around here."

"See!" said Sam. "It works!"

"Pardon me," asked the passenger of the conductor on the railroad train, *"but could you tell me where the town of Fishhook comes?"*

"At the end of the line, of course."

"Is Arizona as healthful as they say?" asked the tourist.

"It certainly is!" replied the native. "Why, when I first came here, I had no hair, I couldn't speak, and I was so weak that they had to carry me around — and look at me now."

"Why, that's remarkable!" said the tourist. "How long ago was that?"

"When I was born!"

Mr. Black was going for his first trip on an airplane, and he was a bit frightened. As the airplane reached two thousand feet, he peeked out of the window.

"Oh, my goodness!" he said, as he looked down at the ground.

When the airplane was up to ten thousand feet, he peeked out of the window again.

"Oh, my gracious!" he said.

When the pilot announced that they were up to twenty thousand feet, he looked out of the window once more.

"Oh, my God!" he exclaimed.

A great voice came back from the clouds:

"YES?"

LADLES AND JELLYSPOONS!

I come before you
to stand behind you
and tell you something
I know nothing about.

Since next Thursday
will be Good Friday,
there will be a father's meeting
for mothers only.

Wear your best clothes,
if you don't have any,
and please stay at home,
if you can be there.

Admission is free.
Pay at the door.
Have a seat on me.
Please sit on the floor.

No matter where you manage to sit,
the man in the balcony will certainly
    spit.

I thank you for your unkind attention
and will now present our next act:

THE FOUR CORNERS OF THE
    ROUND TABLE.

A FLEA AND A FLY FLEW ABOUT
    IN A FLUE.
SAID THE FLY TO THE FLEA,
"WHAT ON EARTH SHALL WE
    DO?"
"SHALL WE FLY?" ASKED THE
    FLEA.
"NO, LET'S FLEE," SAID THE
    FLY.
SO THEY FLUTTERED AND FLEW
    THROUGH A FLAW IN THE
    FLUE.

As a stout lady was walking down Fifth Avenue with her tiny Pekinese dog on a leash, she passed a big moving van parked at the curb. The driver leaned out and yelled at her:

"Hey, lady, could you lend us your Pekinese dog?"

"My good man," replied the lady, "what on earth could you want with my little Fifi?"

"Well, our truck has broken down," explained the man, "and I thought I might use him to tow us to the garage."

"My little Fifi tow that big truck?" said the woman. "My dear sir, you must be quite mad. He is much too small!"

"That's all right, lady," laughed the man. "We've got whips!"

An airplane pilot discovered that a lady he knew had never been up in a plane, so he offered to take her for a ride. In order to make the ride as thrilling as possible for her, he executed a series of loops and spins.

When they had returned to the field, the lady got out of the cockpit very unsteadily and said:

"I'd like to thank you very much for those two rides."

"Two rides?" asked the pilot. "You must still be dizzy. That was only one ride."

"Oh, no!" said the lady. "It was my *first* ride, and it was my *last* ride!"

LADIES AND GENTLEMEN!
May I present here on the palm of my
    hand,
The greatest trained flea in the world,
PRISCILLA!
PRISCILLA DANCES!
Ta-ta te-um-ta.
Ta-ta te-um-ta.
PRISCILLA SINGS!
Oh solo mio.
Oh solo you-oh.
PRISCILLA DOES SOMERSAULTS!
ZOOOOOOOOM!
ZOOOOOOOOOM!
ZOOOOOOOOOM!
YEA, PRISCILLA!
Clap Clap Clap (applause)
UGH-H-H!
POOR PRISCILLA!

A man came into the shoe store and asked the salesman for a pair of shoes one size too small for his feet.

"But why do you want them a size too small?" asked the salesman.

"Because," said the man, "between bills and taxes, and sickness in the family, the only pleasure I have left in life is going home at night and taking off my tight shoes!"

The two secret agents had laid their plans very carefully. They found that the enemy general whom they wanted to assassinate passed a certain corner each morning on the way to his office. They rented a room overlooking the corner and smuggled in several high-powered rifles, a submachine gun, and binoculars.

On the appointed day, they went to the room, got the guns in readiness, and waited for their victim to pass. The usual time came and went, and there was no sign of the enemy general. They were getting more and more nervous.

After half an hour had passed, one of them looked at his watch and said:

"Gosh, he should have been here a long time ago! I hope that nothing's happened to him!"

Little Mabel Moneybags was told by her teacher to write a composition about a poor family. She came up with this classic:

"There once was a very poor family. The mother was poor, the father was poor, and the children were poor. The maid was poor, the governess was poor, the chauffeur was poor, and the butler was poor. They were all frightfully poor!"

A British golfer stepped into a drugstore in America and asked the clerk for something that would be effective against moths. The clerk sold him a box of moth balls. The Britisher returned the next day, then the following one, and a fourth time — each time for another box of moth balls.

The clerk became puzzled as to why he was buying so many, and finally came right out and asked him.

"I say, old man!" replied the Britisher. "You can't expect a chap to hit the little blighters with every shot!"

The same Britisher was walking through the woods with an American friend when they heard a blood-curdling hoot.

"Gor Blimey!" said the Britisher. "What was that?"

"An owl," replied the American.

"Righto, laddie. I know it was an 'owl, but what is doing the 'owling?"

"I've hunted lions and tigers with a rifle," said Hunter Number One.

"I've hunted lions and tigers with a bow and arrow," said Hunter Number Two.

"I've hunted lions and tigers with a club," said Hunter Number Three.

"Good Heavens!" exclaimed the other two. "Weren't you scared?"

"Not at all," replied Hunter Number Three. "There are fifty members in my club!"

A man had been having a dream about a beautiful house in the country. Again and again he would dream about the same house, till he felt that he knew it better than his own. What was his surprise one day, as he was driving his car down a strange road, to see the house of his dreams!

With great excitement he drove up to the front of the house and got out of his car. He went up to the front door and rang the bell. A little old lady answered the ring and opened the door.

"Pardon me, ma'am," said the man, "but this house interests me very much. Could you tell me whether it is for sale?"

"It *is* for sale," said the old lady, "but you wouldn't be interested in buying it."

"Why do you say that?" asked the man.

"Because it's haunted," answered the old lady.

"Haunted?" he asked. "By whom?"

"By you!" said the old lady, closing the door in his face.

Two friends always went fishing together, and one of them always caught all of the fish. One day, the unlucky fisherman decided to go out alone and see if he could do a little better.

He was sitting in the boat in the middle of the lake when he saw a giant bass swimming toward him. Just as he lifted his fishing pole and started to cast, the bass swam right up to the boat and stuck his head out of the water.

"Say, fella," asked the bass, "where's your friend today?"

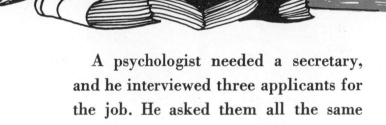

A psychologist needed a secretary, and he interviewed three applicants for the job. He asked them all the same question:

"How much is two and two?"

"Four," answered the first girl.

"Twenty-two," answered the second girl.

"It could be four, or it could be twenty-two," answered the third girl.

Which girl do you think the psychologist hired?

The prettiest one, of course.

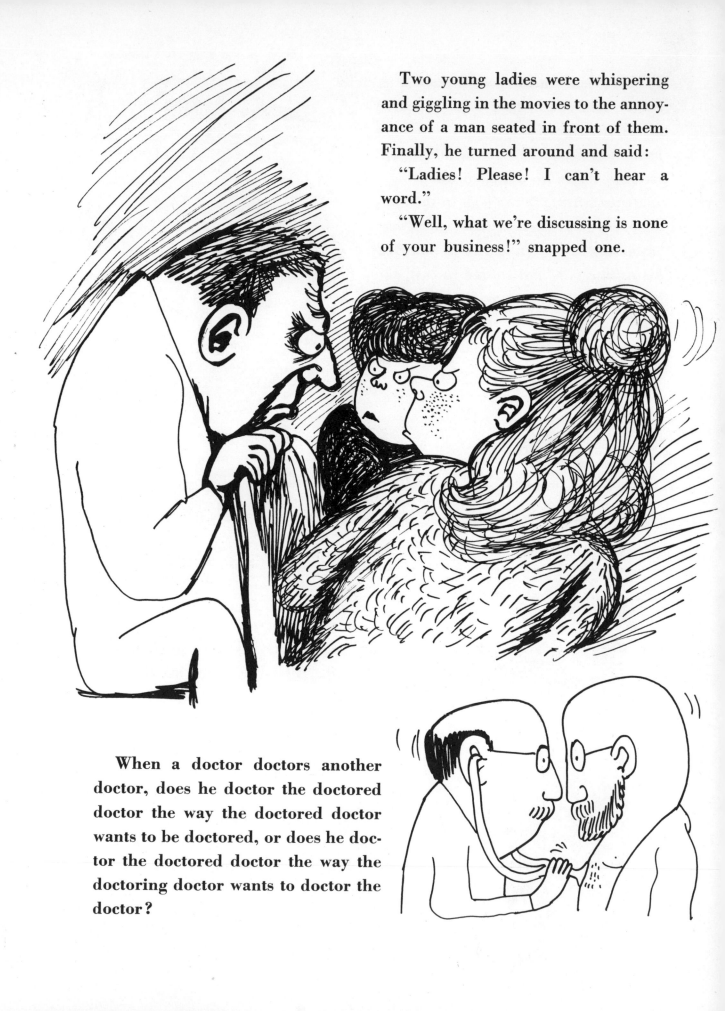

Two young ladies were whispering and giggling in the movies to the annoyance of a man seated in front of them. Finally, he turned around and said:

"Ladies! Please! I can't hear a word."

"Well, what we're discussing is none of your business!" snapped one.

When a doctor doctors another doctor, does he doctor the doctored doctor the way the doctored doctor wants to be doctored, or does he doctor the doctored doctor the way the doctoring doctor wants to doctor the doctor?

Did you hear about poor Sam?

No, what happened?

He fell out of an airplane.

How awful!

Luckily, he wore a parachute.

Oh, good!

Unluckily, the parachute failed to
open.

Horrors!

Luckily, there was a haystack in the
field below.

How fortunate!

Unluckily, there was a sharp pitchfork sticking up in the haystack.

Terrible!

Luckily, he missed the pitchfork.

Thank goodness!

Unluckily, he also missed the
haystack.

Poor Sam!

Poor Mr. Jones was knocked down and run over by a steam roller. When the ambulance returned him to his house, they found that no one was home.

So the attendants simply slipped Mr. Jones under the door.

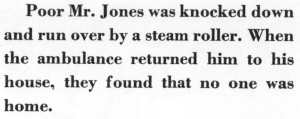

Thaddeus Q. Pinchpenny, the miser, was going over his wife's accounting of her month's expenses.

"Dear," he said, "this extravagance must stop. There is an item of fifty cents for corn plasters, twenty-five cents for aspirin, and three dollars for a tooth extraction.

"That makes three dollars and seventy-five cents that you've squandered on your selfish pleasures!"

In the middle of the show an actor rushed to the front of the stage and shouted, "Is there a doctor in the house?"

A hush fell on the audience, and a man in the tenth row center stood up.

"I am a doctor," he said.

"Hi, Doc," said the actor. "How are you enjoying the show?"

An automobile mechanic had a customer who was always questioning the amount of his bills. One day the customer brought his car to the garage with the complaint that it kept stalling. The mechanic ran the motor, listened to it stall a few times, and took out a wooden mallet. He hit a tube in the motor a few times with the mallet, and then started it again. It ran like a charm.

The next day, the customer got a bill in the mail:

For tapping engine with mallet — One dollar.

For knowing where to tap — Twenty-four dollars.

Total — Twenty-five dollars.

The young man was at a railroad station waiting for his train when he saw the largest, most ornate scale he had ever seen. He had a few minutes, so he stepped on the scale to weigh himself. He was just about to put a penny in,

when he saw the sign: "Weight and Analysis — 10¢"

"Ten cents is a lot of money for a scale," he thought. "But this one looks so fancy, I might as well try it."

So he put a dime in. All of a sudden the scale lit up. The lights started to whirl around. From inside the scale came beautiful music. There was a whirring sound, and a card came out of a slot. The young man picked it up.

It read: "You are five feet ten inches tall, you weigh one hundred sixty-five pounds, you have blue eyes and brown hair, and you are waiting for a train to Chicago."

"Why, this is the most remarkable scale in the whole wide world!" said the young man. "But it is impossible for a scale to know all that. It must be some kind of a trick."

So he stopped a boy who was passing by, and said:

"Son, would you like to make a quarter?"

"Sure," said the boy.

"Then just step on this scale," said the young man.

So the boy stepped on the scale, the young man put another dime in, and again the lights lit up and started to whirl around. Tne music started again, there was the same whirring sound, and another card came out of the slot. The young man grabbed it and read it.

"You are a twelve-year-old boy," read the card. "You are four feet nine inches tall. You have brown eyes and black hair. You are in the seventh grade. And you are here to meet your father."

When the boy had confirmed that all of the information was absolutely true, the young man paid him his quarter. He continued to marvel at the scale. Never had he seen such a wonderful machine!

Finally, he couldn't resist trying it again himself. So he put another dime in the slot. The lights lit up and started to whirl. The beautiful music played. The whirring sound started again. And a card came out of the slot. He read it:

"You are still five feet ten inches tall, you still weigh one hundred sixty-five pounds, you still have blue eyes and brown hair, *but you have just missed your train to Chicago!*"

A restaurateur named Ludwig advertised that he could serve a steak or chop from any animal in the world. One day a customer came into the restaurant and ordered an elephant cutlet.

"I am most regretful, sir," said Ludwig, "but I have only one elephant at the present time and I cannot allow him to be butchered for a single cutlet. Perhaps I can tempt you with a very fine gnu steak. It is most delectable and quite unusual."

The customer agreed, and in a short time he was served with a succulent-looking steak on a sizzling platter.

"That was an excellent steak, Ludwig," he said to his host after he had finished, "but don't think that you have fooled me. I am not certain what animal it came from, but I am sure it was not a gnu."

"I must admit that you are correct, sir," said Ludwig with a twinkle in his eye. "However, you must admit that it was just as good as gnu."

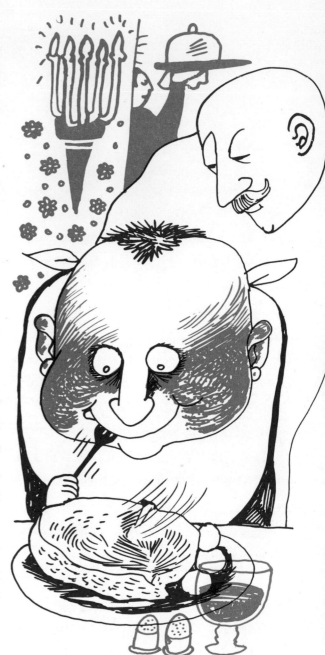

STUDENT: "At school I sleep in a dormitory."
FRIEND: "A what?"
STUDENT: "A dormitory. What did you sleep in when you went to school?"
FRIEND: "My underwear."

SICK JOKES

"*Mommy, Mommy!*
I don't want to go to Europe!"
"*Shut up, and keep swimming!*"

"*Mommy, Mommy!*
I don't want to go to China!"
"*Shut up, and put your other foot in*
the CARE package!"

"*Mommy, Mommy!*
What's a vampire?"
"*Shut up, and eat your soup before it*
clots!"

"Mommy, Mommy!
Daddy's on fire!"
"Quick, get the marshmallows!"

T.B. OR NOT T.B.,
THAT IS THE CONGESTION.
CONSUMPTION BE DONE ABOUT
   IT?
OF COUGH! OF COUGH!

I DON'T CARE WHAT YOUR NAME
   IS, FAT MAN,
GET YOUR REINDEER OFF MY
   ROOF!

I DON'T CARE WHAT YOUR NAME
   IS, LONG EARS,
GET YOUR EGGS OFF MY LAWN!

"My ancestors," boasted the blue-blooded snob, "came over on the May-flower."

"It's a good thing they did," said the fellow he was talking to. "The immigration laws are much stricter now!"

Said one strawberry to the other strawberry: "If you hadn't been such a fool, we wouldn't be in this jam."

"Congratulations!" said the dentist to the rich Texas oilman. "I have examined your teeth thoroughly, and there are absolutely no cavities."

"Can't you drill, anyway, Doc?" asked the oilman. "I feel lucky today!"

An expert criminologist was applying for a new job in the Police Department. One of the members of the board that was examining him asked whether he had had much experience with lie detectors.

"Experience!" snorted the criminologist. "I've been married to one for fifteen years!"

The policeman brought four boys before the judge.

"They caused a terrific commotion at the zoo, your Honor," he said.

"Boys," said the judge sternly, "I never like to hear reports of juvenile delinquency like this. As I point to each one of you, tell me your name, and what you were doing wrong."

"My name is Tom," said the first boy, "and I threw peanuts into the elephant pen."

"My name is Dick," said the second boy, "and I threw peanuts into the elephant pen."

"My name is Harry," said the third boy, "and I threw peanuts into the elephant pen."

"My name is Peanuts," said the fourth boy.

The owner of a large store was awakened by his phone ringing at one o'clock in the morning.

"I'm sorry to bother you," said a sad voice, "but I'd like to know what time you open the store."

"I open the store at ten o'clock!" said the owner angrily, and he banged down the receiver.

About an hour later, just as the owner had again sunk into a deep sleep, the phone rang again.

"I'm sorry to trouble you any more," said the same sad voice. "But don't you ever open the store earlier?"

"No!" shouted the owner. "I never open the store any earlier than ten o'clock. You will have to wait until then to get in!"

"Oh, I don't want to get in," said the sad voice. "I want to get out!"

Why did the pioneers cross the country in covered wagons?

They didn't want to wait forty years for a train or a hundred years for a plane.

HE: "Aren't you ready yet?"
SHE: "I told you an hour ago that I'd be ready in a few minutes."

Paddy was crossing the border when he was stopped by customs agents and asked whether he had anything that was taxable to declare. When he replied in the negative, one of the agents pointed to two gallon jugs on the floor of the car and asked what was in them.

"Why," said Paddy, "they're full of holy water that I'm bringing to the Father at my church."

The agent picked up one of the jugs, unscrewed the top and tasted the contents.

"Hah!" he cried. "It's whiskey!"

"Praise the Saints!" exclaimed Paddy. "It's a miracle!"

It happened somewhere in the Pacific Ocean during World War II. The little fighter plane swooped down to the deck of the giant aircraft carrier. As it came to a stop, the figure of an aviator descended.

The aviator strode to the head of the flight deck and smartly saluted the officer standing there.

"Commander," he said, "I think I deserve a medal or a commendation. I have met and engaged in combat five Japanese planes, and I have shot them all down without making one mistake."

"Oh, so?" hissed the Japanese commander. "Me think you make one mistake!"

Little Willie had just come home from Sunday school, and his mother questioned him about the lessons he had learned that day.

"Well, Ma," he said, "we learned about the time Moses was leading the children of Israel out of Egypt. And how Pharaoh sent his U-2 planes to spot them and then shelled them with rockets and strafed them from jet planes. . .

"And how, when the Israelites got to the Red Sea and thought they were lost, Moses had his engineers put an atom bomb in the bottom of the sea to spread the waters, and then they crossed in safety."

"Why, Willie," said his mother, "I do believe you're fibbing! You couldn't have learned *that* at Sunday school!"

"You're right, Mom," answered Willie. "But if I told you what I *really* learned, you'd never believe me, either!"

As the airliner taxied to a stop, the tourists began to descend toward the waiting natives. The Hawaiians were greeting them with traditional leis, ukuleles, and hula dances.

"Pardon me," asked one tourist of the pretty native who was placing the garland of island flowers around his neck, "but I've always wondered what the correct pronunciation of the name of this beautiful island is. Does one say, HAWAYI, HAWAYA, or HAVAYI?"

"HAVAYI," answered the native with a smile.

"Thank you very much," said the tourist.

"You're velcome," was the reply.

The motorcycle policeman dismounted and walked back to the car he had flagged over to the side of the road.

"Okay, Bud," he said, as he pulled out his book of tickets. "Speeding, going through two red lights, driving on the wrong side of the road, and failing to stop when I signaled you. Do you have anything to say to that?"

The poor driver just sat there, but his wife leaned over and spoke to the officer very sweetly.

"You'll have to excuse him today," she said. "He's as drunk as he can be!"

The New Yorker was showing his guest from Texas around the city, but the Texan wasn't very impressed. Every tall building he saw reminded him of a bigger and better building in Texas — and not only that, he recounted how the buildings in Texas had been built in a matter of months or weeks.

"Why, look at that big department store over there," he said. "We have one in Dallas five times as big, and they put it up in three weeks."

This went on and on, hour after hour, and the New Yorker was getting very annoyed. Suddenly they came within sight of the Empire State Building.

"Wow!" exclaimed the Texan. "What's that big building over there?"

The New Yorker looked bored.

"Gosh," he said, "I don't know — it wasn't there yesterday!"

Mr. Fish, the great chess expert, had a Japanese houseboy who performed all of his duties admirably. The servant, however, did have an annoying habit of interrupting his employer during chess games to ask about the smallest household problems.

Finally, the exasperated Mr. Fish had to lecture the houseboy most severely and threatened to discharge him if he ever interrupted a chess game again.

One day, as a chess game was in progress, the houseboy came into the room and stood there bowing and smiling but not saying anything. After a half-hour, when the game was concluded, Mr. Fish looked up at him approvingly and said:

"All right, Tojo, I see that you have learned your lesson. Now what is it that you wanted?"

"Only desire to inform honorable sir, please," replied the grinning houseboy, "that house is on fire!"

The farmer had a son who went to the city where he opened a shoeshine parlor. Now the farmer makes hay while the son shines.

The would-be big shot was trying to impress his girl friend.

"Waiter!" he commanded. "Bring us two orders of Aldo Bruschi."

"I beg your pardon, sir," said the waiter, "but he's the proprietor!"

The sales manager came in to see the boss.

"I'd like you to get rid of that salesman we hired last month," he said. "He refuses to take orders, and yesterday, when I told him I was going to report him to you, he said that both of us could jump in the lake."

"Let me see his sales record," said the boss, and when it was brought to him, he studied it carefully. "I see that he's sold over a million dollars worth of goods since he's been with us."

"I know," said the sales manager, "but he insists on doing everything his own way, and if you don't like it, he tells you to go jump in the lake. What do you think we should do about it?"

"I don't know what you plan to do," said the boss, "but I figure I can always get a new suit."

Sweeney was hired as a bus driver, and to break him in, he was put on one of the easiest runs in town — the Seventy-second Street Crosstown. He carried few passengers, and most days the receipts averaged less than six dollars.

One day he was three hours late returning to the garage. The dispatcher was just about to turn in a police alarm for him, when in walked Sweeney.

"Where have you been?" asked the frantic dispatcher.

"Oh," said Sweeney as he dumped about fifty dollars on the dispatcher's desk, "business was so bad on Seventy-second Street, that I took the bus up Broadway today!"

The agent from the Bureau of Internal Revenue came into the Italian grocery store and said to the proprietor:

"Mr. Salerno, I've come to see you about taxes."

"Sure," said Mr. Salerno. "I know alla 'bout taxes—datsa where my friend Pietro he live."

"No, no," said the agent, "I don't mean Texas — I'm referring to the dollars you owe the government."

"Datsa right, datsa right," said Salerno. "My friend Pietro, he live in Dallas, Texas!"

FIRST STUDENT: "How did you like those examination questions?"

SECOND STUDENT: "The questions didn't give me any trouble — it was the answers that were hard."

A salesman came to call on the purchasing agent of a large corporation. The purchasing agent detected a slight foreign accent in the salesman's speech, and told him that it was the policy of the firm to buy only from American suppliers. The salesman hastened to reassure the purchasing agent that he had been brought up in Europe only because his father had been the American ambassador to many foreign countries, and that his family could be traced back to the Mayflower.

On that basis, the two concluded a highly profitable — for the salesman — session. As the salesman was closing his brief case, he looked at a picture of Abraham Lincoln hanging on the wall.

"Fine-looking gentleman," he said. "President of the company?"

An insurance salesman was trying to sell an accident policy to a reluctant prospect.

"Take the case of Mr. Mifoofsky," he said. "Three days after I sold him a policy, he was in an accident and he lost an arm and a leg."

"I know," said the reluctant prospect. "But he was one of the lucky ones!"

The Scotsman was walking along the boardwalk at the seashore with a lady friend.

"Ummm!" she hinted. "Don't those hamburgers smell delicious?"

"Well," he answered, "we can walk back and you can get a better smell at them."

Mrs. Smith was admiring her new vicuña coat.

"Just think," she said to her friend. "The animals that were shorn for this coat lived in South America, the fabric was woven in England, and the coat was finished in New York!"

"What's so remarkable about that?" asked her friend.

"So many people have made a living out of this coat," she replied, "and I haven't even paid for it yet!"

George received an anonymous letter in the mail that read: "You'd better stop stealing my chickens or I'm going to shoot you dead!"

He quickly went to the police station and showed the threatening letter to the officer there.

"Well," laughed the officer, "it seems simple enough. All you have to do is stop stealing those chickens."

"But this letter ain't signed!" protested George. "I don't know whose chickens I'm supposed to stop stealing!"

One day the lion was stalking through the jungle, roaring his mighty roar.

"WHO IS KING OF THE JUNGLE?" he roared.

"You are, oh mighty lion!" chorused the pack of jackals at his heels.

The lion came upon an ape, cowering in his path. The lion lifted his paw, bared his fangs, and roared:

"WHO IS KING OF THE JUNGLE?"

"You are, oh mighty lion!" whimpered the ape.

The lion stalked further, and he came upon a tiger.

"WHO IS KING OF THE JUNGLE?" he asked.

The tiger stood his ground, arched his back, and snarled back at the lion.

With one mighty leap, the lion landed on top of the tiger. He cuffed him with his mighty paw, and held his teeth near the tiger's throat.

"WHO IS KING OF THE JUNGLE?" he growled.

"You are, oh mighty lion," said the tiger, and the lion let him up and he slunk away.

As the lion got to the water hole in the jungle, he met an elephant.

"WHO IS KING OF THE JUNGLE?" roared the lion.

The elephant ignored him, and lumbered on.

"WHO IS KING OF THE JUNGLE?" screamed the lion.

The elephant merely lifted one of his great forelegs and placed it on the lion's back. Then he wrapped his trunk around the lion's body and raised him into the air. Finally, he walked over to the water hole and dropped the lion in.

"You don't have to get so angry," sputtered the lion as he dragged himself out of the water, "just because you don't know the answer to my question."

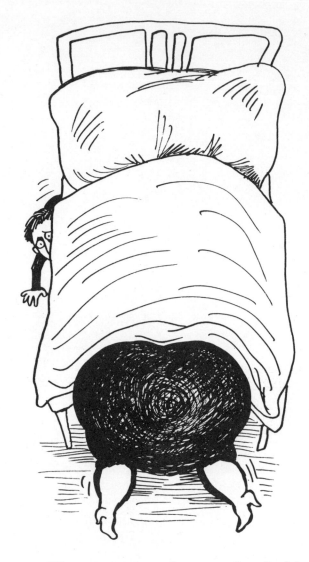

Maggie and Jiggs were always fighting, and their fights usually ended with Jiggs getting a few well-placed blows from Maggie's rolling pin.

Thus it was with considerable amazement that one of their neighbors saw Jiggs strolling down the street without his usual black eye or lump on the head.

"Didn't you and Maggie fight last night?" asked the neighbor.

"We sure did!" said Jiggs.

"Well, how did it turn out?" asked the neighbor.

"Why, she came to me on her hands and knees," said Jiggs.

"Really!" said the neighbor. "What did she say?"

" 'Come out from under that bed, you coward!' "

The manager of a men's clothing store was interviewing a candidate for a job as a salesman.

"Now we need real high-pressure selling in this store," he said to the applicant. "Do you think that you have the proper background?"

"Well," answered the prospective salesman, "all I can tell you is that on my last job I had a woman come in to buy a suit to bury her husband in — and I ended up selling her an extra pair of pants and a sports jacket!"

One of the stands at Coney Island was found to be watering its orange juice, adding fat to the hamburgers, and, in short, doing everything possible to sell a little for a lot. In court, the owner of the stand pleaded that he was not putting anything harmful into his products, and that customers would not suffer from eating them, but the judge stood on the law. "You must tell the truth about everything you sell!" he said.

The happy ending of the story is that the owner obeyed the law, and yet his business doubled. He put up a big sign that read:

EVERYTHING YOU EAT OR
DRINK AT THIS STAND IS
WARRANTED TO BE
ADULTERATED AS MUCH
AS POSSIBLE.

Sandy invited a friend to his house for a birthday party, and gave detailed directions for getting there. After he had finished, he said:

"And when you come to the door, push the bell with your elbow. When the buzzer sounds, push the door open with your foot."

"I understand the directions perfectly," said the friend. "But why must I push the bell with my elbow and open the door with my foot?"

"Hoot, mon!" said Sandy. "I hope you are not planning to come to the party empty-handed!"

Tim used to come home drunk almost every night. Hoping to cure him of this habit, his wife put on a white sheet one night and waited for him at the street corner.

"Tim!" she said in a low voice, as he staggered toward her. "I have come to get you."

"And who are you?" asked Tim.

"I am the Devil!" she answered in a scary voice.

"Then I am glad to meet you," said Tim. "I've been married to your sister for the past twenty-five years!"

Pat had been boasting to Mike about his wonderful thoroughbred police dog. One day Mike finally saw the dog. It turned out to be nothing more than a mangy-looking mongrel.

"Whisht, Pat!" he said. "That cur is no more police dog than I am!"

"Sh, Mike!" whispered Pat. "Didn't I tell you? He's on the Plainclothes Squad!"

Chickens had been mysteriously disappearing from Farmer Brown's henhouse. He suspected a chicken thief, and so he slept with his shotgun next to his bed, and one eye and ear open.

On a certain moonlit night he heard a stealthy tread outside. He jumped up and looked out the window. There in the yard he saw a furtive shadow slinking toward the henhouse.

Farmer Brown grabbed his trusty shotgun. He ran down the stairs, into the yard, and toward the henhouse.

Putting his shotgun to his shoulder, he called out, "Whoever is in there, come out!"

A small, frightened voice came back from out of the henhouse:

"There's nobody in here but us chickens!"

Swami, the great magician, used to love rabbit stew. One day, as he was enjoying his favorite dish in a restaurant, he found that this particular stew was not agreeing with him. First he turned pale, and then he turned green. Finally, he threw his napkin down and ran as fast as he could toward the washroom.

"Well," observed a waiter, "that's the first time a rabbit ever made a magician disappear!"

A miserly miserable old millionaire finally died, and he went up to the Pearly Gates of Heaven and banged on them.

"Who comes here, with such a loud noise?" demanded Saint Peter.

"Let me in!" cried the millionaire.

"Who are you?" asked Peter.

"I am a millionaire," said the millionaire.

"That doesn't mean anything up here," said Peter. "What good works or deeds did you ever do on earth that we should admit you?"

"Last year I gave a dollar to a poor old crippled woman who was begging," said the millionaire.

"Is that correct, Gabriel?" asked Saint Peter of the angel.

"Yes, it is," replied Gabriel. "Here it is in the book: 'Gave one dollar to poor old crippled woman.'"

"What else did you do?" asked Peter.

"About five years ago I gave two dollars to charity," said the millionaire.

"Is that true, Gabriel?" asked Peter.

Gabriel looked it up in the book. "Yes, it is," he said.

"Well, Gabriel," said Peter, "what do you think we ought to do with this fellow?"

"Give him back his three dollars," said Gabriel, "and let him go to the Devil!"

The machinist at the factory took his lunch box over to a bench each day and sat down to eat. He would open the lid just an inch and peek in expectantly. And every day, when he saw what was inside, his face would fall and he would mutter:

"Nuts! Peanut butter again!"

After this had gone on for several months, his neighbor spoke to him:

"If you don't like peanut butter sandwiches, why don't you ask your wife to make you something else?"

"Oh, I'm not married," said the machinist. "I make these every morning, myself!"

Two Russians were seated in a cafe, staring moodily at their glasses of tea. After a while, one of them spoke to the other:

"Igor Igorovich," he said, "why is life like a glass of tea?"

The other one thought and thought, and a puzzled look came over his face.

"Vassily Vassilivich," he said, "I don't know. Tell me, why is life like a glass of tea?"

There was another long pause, and finally the first one shrugged his shoulders.

"How should I know?" he asked. "Am I a philosopher?"

Two Boy Scouts were out on their first overnight hike and found it somewhat difficult snuggling down in their sleeping bags so that the mosquitoes wouldn't get at them. After a while one of them saw some fireflies flying about and he said to his friend:

"We might as well give up, George — those mosquitoes are looking for us with flashlights, now!"

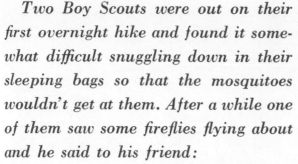

"Your Honor," said the man, "I must have a divorce. I cannot stand to live in the same house with my wife any longer. She keeps a pet pig, and the odor is driving me out of my mind."

"I'll admit that is somewhat of a difficulty," replied the judge, "but couldn't you consider keeping the windows open to get rid of the smell?"

"What!" said the man. "And let all of my pet bats fly out?"

Mr. Howard had a dog who was very smart. As a matter of fact, this dog was so smart that Mr. Howard sent him away to college. When the dog returned from college, Mr. Howard asked him how he had fared in his studies.

"I didn't do very well in mathematics," said the dog, "but I got very good marks in foreign languages."

"Well, then," said Mr. Howard, "let's hear you say something in a foreign language."

"MEOW!" said the dog.

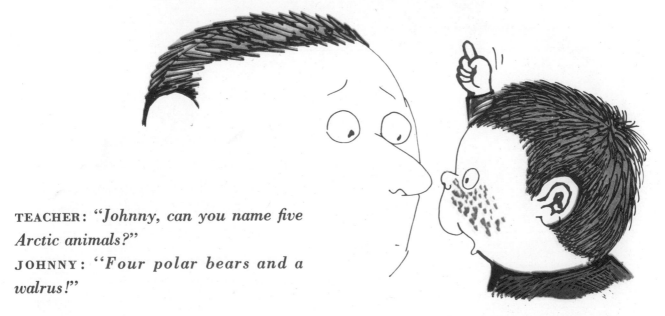

TEACHER: *"Johnny, can you name five Arctic animals?"*
JOHNNY: *"Four polar bears and a walrus!"*

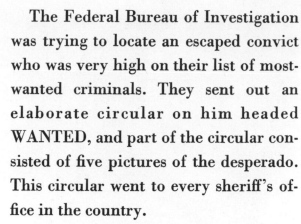

The Federal Bureau of Investigation was trying to locate an escaped convict who was very high on their list of most-wanted criminals. They sent out an elaborate circular on him headed WANTED, and part of the circular consisted of five pictures of the desperado. This circular went to every sheriff's office in the country.

About a week later, the main office received the following telegram from a newly elected sheriff in Nevada who was trying to make a name for himself as quickly as possible:

"HAVE RECEIVED PICTURES OF THE FIVE MOST-WANTED CRIMINALS STOP FOUR ARE ALREADY UNDER ARREST STOP HOT ON THE TRAIL OF THE FIFTH ONE STOP."

A man went on his first airplane trip, and when he got to his destination, his friend asked him how he had enjoyed it.

"It was nice," said the man. "I had only one bit of trouble."

"What was that?" asked the friend.

"Well," said the man, "when we started, the stewardess handed me a piece of chewing gum, and told me it was for my ears. It worked fine for the noise and everything, but I had a very hard time getting it out of my ears after we landed!"

The angel Gabriel and Saint Peter had an argument about which of them was the better golfer, and they decided to settle it with a golf match on earth. Saint Peter swung at the ball on the very first tee and sliced it badly into a clump of trees. But just before it hit a tree, a hawk swooped down and grabbed the ball in its beak. The hawk flew over the green where it dropped the ball. As the ball was bouncing on the green, a rabbit darted along and pushed it right into the hole.

"All right, Pete," said the angel Gabriel, "stop fooling around with the miracles and let's play a little golf!"

Mrs. Dogood was appointed to the board of a privately endowed home for wayward boys. Her appointment was made because the other directors expected her to make a sizable donation to the home each year, but Mrs. Dogood insisted upon working at the job. She started off by visiting the home several times a week and interviewing all of the inmates.

"Gentlemen," she announced at the first board meeting that she attended after her survey, "I think our main problem is that we must attract a better class of boys to this institution!"

The children of the nursery class had just gotten settled, and the teacher made a quick inspection of the coat-room. There, on the floor, she saw a telltale puddle. Straightaway, she walked to the front of the classroom.

"Now, children," she said, "someone has had a little accident in the coat-room, and I want the person responsible to step forward at once."

No one moved.

"Come, now, children," said the teacher, sitting down at her desk. "Perhaps we can handle this in another way. We will all close our eyes for three minutes, and in that time the person who is responsible can go to the coat-room, clean up the puddle with a paper towel, and then the damage will be all repaired and no one will know who it was."

So they all closed their eyes tightly.

There was a patter of little feet . . . then silence . . . then the patter of little feet again . . . then silence.

"All right, children," said the teacher. "We can all open our eyes again."

As they did so, she got up with a smile on her face and walked to the coat-room. She looked into the coat-room and the smile came right off her face.

For there on the floor was the same puddle. And next to it was another puddle. And next to that was a piece of paper with the inscription, "THE PHANTOM STRIKES AGAIN!"

McTavish had taken his family to Coney Island for the day, and they were all exhausted as they started home, so McTavish approached a taxicab and spoke to the driver.

"How much would you charge to take my wife, my four children and me, to the Bronx?" he asked.

"Well," replied the taxi driver, "I figure three dollars each for you and your wife, and the kids can ride for nothing."

"Fine!" said McTavish, as he herded his four children into the taxicab. "You children have a nice ride home. Mother and I are taking the subway!"

TAXI

MOE: "How are you, Joe? I haven't seen you in years!"

JOE: "I just got married."

MOE: "That's wonderful!"

JOE: "No, it isn't. My wife is the ugliest girl in the world."

MOE: "That's terrible!"

JOE: "No, it isn't. She has a hundred million dollars."

MOE: "That's wonderful!"

JOE: "No, it isn't. She squeezes a nickel till the buffalo bellows."

MOE: "That's terrible!"

JOE: "No, it isn't. She owns a beautiful estate in the country with a fifty-room house on it."

MOE: "That's wonderful!"

JOE: "No, it isn't. The house burned down to the ground last night."

MOE: "That's terrible!"

JOE: "No, it isn't. My wife was in it!"

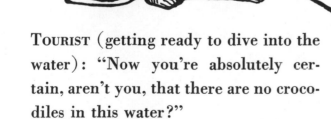

TOURIST (getting ready to dive into the water): "Now you're absolutely certain, aren't you, that there are no crocodiles in this water?"

NATIVE: "Positive, sir — the sharks have scared them all away."

Lou Simon became very much distressed because he felt that his friends doubted his veracity when it came to stories about the fish he had caught. Because of this, he purchased an elaborate set of brass scales, which he placed in his home, and when he made a particularly momentous catch, he would invite friends over for cocktails and weigh the fish in their presence.

One night, as he was having such a fish-weighing party, a neighbor from down the street burst in and asked to borrow the scales for a few minutes. This was done.

About twenty minutes later, the excited neighbor returned with the scales and shouted:

"Congratulate me, everybody! My wife has just given birth to a fifty-six pound girl!"

Patient: "Doctor, my wooden leg is giving me a lot of pain."

Doctor: "That is very unusual. I wonder why?"

Patient: "My wife hit me over the head with it."

Every time the plane from New York to Los Angeles stopped at an airport, a little blue car raced up to refuel it.

"This plane certainly makes good time," said one passenger.

"It sure does," answered the other, "but that little blue car seems to keep right up with it!"

The minister was visiting a miser in the hospital. The miser thought that he was going to die, and he begged the minister to pray for him.

"If I recover," he promised, "I will give a new organ to the church."

Months after the miser had made a miraculous recovery, the minister became tired of waiting for the promised donation and he went to the miser's home.

"You promised to donate a new organ to the church if you recovered," he reminded the miser. "Now that you have recovered, you seem to have forgotten your promise."

"Oh, my goodness!" said the miser. "Did I really promise a thing like that? It just goes to show how deathly ill I was. I must have been delirious and out of my mind!"

MOE: *"Why so glum, Joe?"*
JOE: *"My wife went to the race track."*
MOE: *"How did she make out?"*
JOE: *"She lost four races."*
MOE: *"Don't be so sad. Why, I doubt if my wife could even run around the track once!"*

The explorer had been captured by cannibals several times, but each time they had released him, and he had gone on to new expeditions. Finally, after he had retired, he disclosed the secret of his success. Whenever the cannibals started boiling the pot to cook him in, he would say to the chief:

"I gather you are planning to eat me for dinner. I assure you that you will not enjoy it."

Thereupon he would reach down with a knife and cut a piece out of his leg which he would present to the chief — who would always release him.

The explorer had a wooden leg!

Captain John Smith went through three horrible years of war, and the only thing that sustained him during that time was the love he had for a girl back home. What was his surprise and chagrin to get a letter from his love, saying she was going to marry someone else, and she wanted her picture returned.

In his misery, he obtained as many pictures of other women as he could lay his hands on. He put them all into a big package, and enclosed this note:

Dear What's-your-name:

I don't remember which picture is yours, but if you will pick it out and send the rest back to me, I will be,

Yours sincerely,
John.

The diner called the waiter:
"Would you kindly close the window?" he said. "I'm afraid my steak is going to blow away."

JUDGE: "Mr. Smith, you have not lived up to your marriage obligations at all. I am going to award your wife one hundred dollars a month for her support."

SMITH: "That's very kind of you, Judge, and I'll try to send her a few dollars, myself."

Mr. Malaprop was writing an important order to his butcher for his New Year's geese, but he was having difficulty expressing himself.

"Please send me my New Year's gooses . . ." he started.

"Please send me my New Year's geeses . . ." he amended.

Finally he began all over again and wrote:

"Please send me my New Year's goose.

"P.S. — And while you're at it, send another one."

The summer resident came into the general store with a mail-order catalogue in his hand.

"Do you carry a hammer like that?" he asked the storekeeper, pointing to a picture in the catalogue.

"I reckon so," replied the storekeeper, and he went to the back of the store and came back with a hammer just like the one in the picture. "That'll be a dollar and a half," he added as he started to wrap the hammer.

"But look here," said the summer resident. "The price of this hammer in the mail-order catalogue is a dollar and a quarter."

"Well, now, I reckon we have to meet the competition," said the storekeeper, "so you can have the hammer for a dollar and a quarter. But you would have to pay twenty-two cents postage if you ordered it from that catalogue, so it will come to a dollar forty-seven cents, anyway."

"Ha, ha!" laughed the summer resident. "I guess you have me there." And he counted out a dollar and forty-seven cents.

Just as he reached for the package, however, the storekeeper took it and placed it on a shelf behind the counter.

"You can come by in three weeks and pick it up," said the storekeeper. "That's how long it would take to come from the mail-order house."

Doctor Garn had done a great deal of dental work for a patient, but had never gotten paid. One day he decided to go and see the patient and collect the bill. When he returned, his wife took one look at him and said, "I can tell that you didn't collect the money that was owed you."

"Not only that," he answered, "but I was bitten by my own teeth!"

The new convict was sent to the prison barber shop on his first day, so that his hair might be shaved off, according to regulations. The prisoner was miserable about being where he was, he was also unhappy about having his scalp shaved, and to top it all, the prison barber was the most annoyingly talkative man imaginable. For twenty minutes, as he was using his razor, the barber kept up a constant stream of small talk about anything and everything. Just as he was finished, he spoke to the convict.

"Say," he said, "you're new around here. What did you get sent up for?"

The convict looked at the barber menacingly.

"My old barber used to talk too much," he said, "so one day I grabbed the scissors from him and stabbed him!"

The annual office picnic was on a Sunday, and Jones really had a good time. He drank too freely, however, and when he woke up he couldn't remember much of what had happened. He struggled into the office about an hour late and during the day got several cold looks from his boss. Finally he could stand the fish-eye treatment no longer, and he spoke to the boss.

"Don't you think you're making a mountain out of a molehill," he asked, "just because I was an hour late this morning?"

"Oh, I don't mind the hour *this* morning," replied the boss, "but I'd like to know where you were Monday and Tuesday!"

The chemistry teacher had a beaker of acid on the bench in front of him. He held a half dollar in his hand and spoke to the class.

"Now I will drop this half dollar into this acid. Can anyone tell me whether or not it will dissolve?"

"It will not dissolve," spoke up one student.

"That is correct. Now can you tell me the reason you think it will not dissolve?"

"Because," replied the student, "if it would dissolve, you wouldn't drop it in!"

Two cockroaches found their way into a brand new building. They went from apartment to apartment, and could hardly find a crumb to devour. Finally they came across a big piece of cake that someone had left out on a kitchen table.

As they were munching away on the cake, one roach said to the other:

"These new buildings are a real problem. Everything is so clean and shiny and sanitary."

"Please!" answered his fellow cockroach. "Don't talk like that. Can't you see that I'm eating?"

The drill sergeant was finding particular fault with one of the new draftees. After bawling him out several times during the morning he finally exploded:

"You are the most incompetent human being I have ever come across. Just what were you in civilian life?"

The answer came back quickly: "Happy."

WIFE: "I wait on my husband hand and foot. Whenever he sews buttons or darns his socks, I have to thread the needle for him."

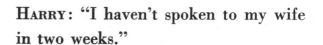

HARRY: "I haven't spoken to my wife in two weeks."
DICK: "How come?"
HARRY: "I don't like to interrupt her."

TOM: "I wonder why Bob takes his wife on all of his business trips."
SAM: "It's easier than kissing her good-by."

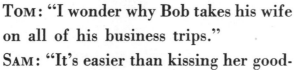

GALLAGHER: "Those oysters your wife ate at the restaurant last night didn't look too good. Did they disagree with her?"
SHEAN: "They wouldn't dare!"

MOTHER: "Dear, I think that we should buy Jackie an encyclopedia."

FATHER: "What does he need an encyclopedia for?"

MOTHER: "Why, for school, of course."

FATHER: "That's too bad about him. Let him walk to school, just as I did!"

Farmer Jones planted his onions and potatoes next to each other in a field. He figured that the onions would make the potatoes' eyes water, and he wouldn't have to bother about irrigation.

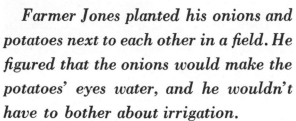

Mr. Greeble says that his wife's biggest talent is doing bird imitations. She watches him like a hawk, talks like a magpie, eats like a vulture, and has the disposition of an old buzzard.

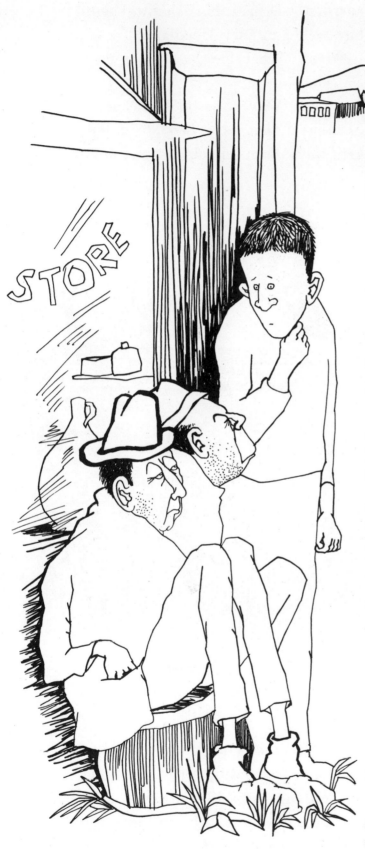

The summer resident walked up to the general store one day. The storekeeper and a few of his cronies were sitting in front of the store, chatting and whittling.

"Do you have any three-inch nails?" asked the summer resident.

"Well, I reckon you might find a keg of them back on the counter," said the storekeeper as he spit some tobacco juice in the ground.

The summer resident went into the store and looked on the counter, but he could find no keg of three-inch nails. Then he looked all over the rest of the store, but he couldn't find a keg of three-inch nails anywhere. He went back outside, but just as he was about to tell the storekeeper of his fruitless search, his eye spotted something.

"Why, look, Zeke," he said to the storekeeper. "That keg you're sitting on — *that's* a keg of three-inch nails!"

Zeke kept on whittling, he spat out some tobacco juice, and he lazily looked down at the side of the keg he was sitting on.

"Reckon you're right," he said. "I guess you'll just have to come back tomorrow!"

Mother Turtle, Father Turtle, and Baby Turtle were sitting down for dinner one night when Mother Turtle discovered that she had forgotten to buy coffee at the store that day.

"I'll go to the store and get it," said Baby Turtle, and he started out.

A little while later, Father Turtle spoke to Mother Turtle.

"Where is that young one? He should be getting back from the store by now!"

"I know," replied Mother Turtle, "I'm beginning to think that he's not very dependable."

Just then a voice floated in from the window:

"If you two don't stop talking about me, I'm not going to go at all!"

A man came running into a drug store and breathlessly said to the pharmacist:

"Quick, I need something to cure hiccups!"

The pharmacist walked around to the front of the counter and slapped the man on the back as hard as he could.

"Why did you do that?" gasped the man.

"Well, you don't have hiccups any more!" replied the pharmacist smugly.

"I never had them," replied the man. "My *wife* has them and I needed something to cure her!"

The chief electrician and his assistant were working on a very complicated job. All of a sudden the chief stopped his work and looked at two wires sticking out of the panel. One was black and the other was white. He thought a minute, scratched his head, and said to his assistant:

"Bill, grab that black wire."

The assistant did as he was told, and then the chief asked, "Do you feel anything?"

"No," answered the assistant.

"Good!" said the chief. "I was wondering which was which. Now, for heaven's sake, don't touch that white one — it will kill you!"

"Hello! Is this the office of Livingston, Livingston, Livingston and Livingston, Attorneys-at-Law?"

"Yes, it is."

"May I speak with Mr. Livingston, please?"

"Sorry, he's in court."

"May I speak with Mr. Livingston, please?"

"Sorry, he's in conference."

"May I speak with Mr. Livingston, please?"

"Sorry, he's on vacation."

"May I speak with Mr. Livingston, please?"

"Speaking."

An old maid fell in love with the statue of a Confederate general mounted on a horse. Every day she would pass the statue and look longingly and admiringly at the handsome, dashing figure of her dream man. One day, as she was standing in front of the statue, a good fairy appeared before her and spoke.

"I am your good fairy," said the good fairy, "and I have come to grant you any two wishes your heart may desire."

"Oh, thank you," said the old maid. "My first wish will be to bring the statue of the general to life, because I love him so. And my second wish I will give to the general, so that he may have whatever he wants most, too."

Thereupon, the good fairy brought the statue of the general to life, and the old maid explained to him exactly what had happened.

"I have given you life," she concluded, "and now you may also have any wish fulfilled."

"Ma'am," replied the general, "I do not want you to think me ungrateful, but you must realize that my statue has been standing in this park for more than fifty years. So please try and understand when I tell you that my greatest wish is to shoot a million pigeons!"

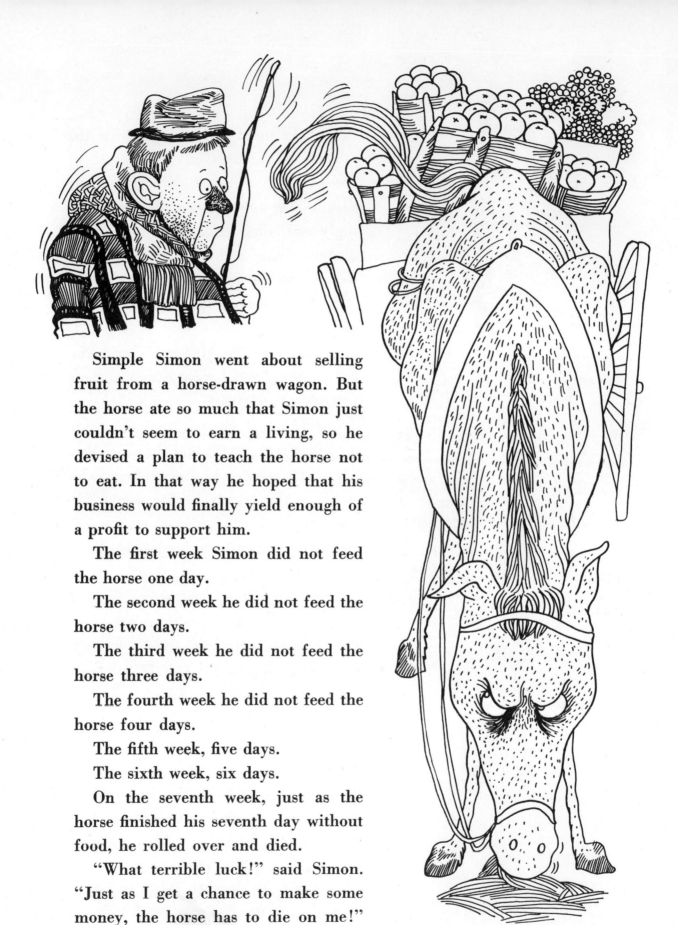

Simple Simon went about selling fruit from a horse-drawn wagon. But the horse ate so much that Simon just couldn't seem to earn a living, so he devised a plan to teach the horse not to eat. In that way he hoped that his business would finally yield enough of a profit to support him.

The first week Simon did not feed the horse one day.

The second week he did not feed the horse two days.

The third week he did not feed the horse three days.

The fourth week he did not feed the horse four days.

The fifth week, five days.

The sixth week, six days.

On the seventh week, just as the horse finished his seventh day without food, he rolled over and died.

"What terrible luck!" said Simon. "Just as I get a chance to make some money, the horse has to die on me!"

RIDDLES

Why did Silly Billy bring a ladder to school?

Because he wanted to go to high school.

Why did Silly Billy jump off the Empire State building?

Because he wanted to make a hit on Broadway.

Why did Silly Billy throw the clock out the window?

Because he wanted to see time fly.

Why did Silly Billy keep running around his bed?

Because he wanted to catch up on his sleep.

Why did Silly Billy drive his car off the cliff?

Because he wanted to try out the new air brakes.

Why was Silly Billy skipping rope?
Because he had just taken his medi-cine, and he forgot to shake the bottle.

Why did Silly Billy stand in back of the mule?

Because he thought he might get a kick out of it.

Why did Silly Billy buy chewing gum on the train?

Because he heard the engine say, "Choo-Choo."

Why did Silly Billy laugh up his sleeve?

Because that is where his "funny bone" is.

Why did the Silly Billy sew labels marked "cotton" in all of his woolen clothing?

To fool the moths.

Why did Silly Billy go to the barber?
Because he couldn't stand his hair any longer.

Why did Silly Billy close the refrigerator door?

Because the mayonnaise was dressing.

Why did Silly Billy tiptoe past the medicine cabinet?
To avoid waking the sleeping pills.

Why do they name hurricanes after girls? Like Ada, Beth, Clara, Dora, etc.?
Because they're not himicanes.

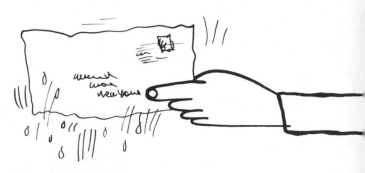

Why did Silly Billy drive around the corner on two wheels?
To save wear on his tires.

Why did the letter arrive wet?
There was postage dew.

What shape is a present?
I don't know.
Just give me one and we'll call it square.

Why couldn't that milkmaid milk the cow?
Because she has no regard for the feeling of udders.

Where is the fencing master?
Out to lunge.

Mr. Jordan died, and shortly thereafter his spirit arrived at the gates of Heaven. Saint Peter asked him his name, looked at the list of arrivals and said:

"I am sorry, Mr. Jordan, but you are not on our list. I am very much afraid that you have come to the wrong place."

So Mr. Jordan tearfully set out for the lower regions, and he soon came to the gates of Hell. Here the gatekeeper of the Devil asked his name and looked at the list. Again Mr. Jordan's name was not on the list.

Hopefully, now, Mr. Jordan returned to the Pearly Gates and told Saint Peter that he was not on the list at the other place.

"How very strange!" said Saint Peter. "We will have to check up on this at the main office. You had better have a seat, meanwhile, and I will let you know when I have the information."

Mr. Jordan sat and waited nervously. About an hour later, Saint Peter came over to him and said:

"Mr. Jordan, there has been a horrible mistake. According to our records at the main office, you were not supposed to die for another ten years. Mr. Jordan, *who is your doctor?*"

PROUD PARENT: "Johnny is studying French, German, and Algebra in school."
GROUCHY UNCLE: "Let's hear him say something in Algebra."

After many years, McSweeny decided to have his saloon redecorated, and he closed the place down for a month to do a thorough job. Everything was brand new and very elegant, and all of the customers were delighted. Only one old-timer had a minor complaint.

"McSweeny," he said, "I miss that big brass spittoon you had right in front of the bar."

"I'm not surprised," said McSweeny. "You missed it for ten years when it was here!"

One day a kangaroo hopped into a bar, hopped up on a stool, and ordered a glass of beer. The bartender looked a bit startled, then started to draw the beer.

"You know," said the bartender, "this is the first time I have ever seen a kangaroo in a bar. Did you know that there is a drink named after you?"

"Really?" asked the kangaroo. "A drink named Cecil?"

"Mommy, Mommy!" yelled little Joseph. "There's a dog outside, and he's bigger than a truck!"

"Now, Joseph," said his mother. "You know I've told you a thousand million times not to exaggerate!"

Nervous old lady to stewardess on airliner: "Miss, do these big jets crash very often?"

Stewardess: "Oh, my, no! Only once!"

ED: "When I married, I got a real prize."
FRED: "That so? What was it?"

They told me that it couldn't be done.
But I grinned and went right to it.
I tackled the job that couldn't be done.
And, by gosh, I couldn't do it!

The Scotsman dined well at the restaurant, but the waiter turned his nose up at the five-cent tip that he left.

"What's the matter, laddie?" asked the Scotsman, noting the grieved look.

"Well," said the waiter, "even the champion miser in the city leaves a dime tip when he eats here."

"Well, laddie," said the Scotsman, "you're looking at the new champion."

A factory produced some very valuable articles, and there were elaborate precautions taken to see that none of the workmen stole anything.

Every day at lunchtime, a workman would appear at one of the gates, pushing a wheelbarrow full of rubbish. The guards were very suspicious of him and they always searched through the rubbish. But they never found anything of value — only rubbish. So they always had to let him pass through.

This went on every day for several years, and then the plant closed down.

A short time thereafter, one of the guards passed the former workman. He was dressed very elegantly, and just getting into a sporty new car.

"Aha!" said the guard. "I always knew you were stealing something, even though we never caught you. Now that it's too late for me to do anything about it, how about satisfying my curiosity and telling me what it was you were stealing."

"Sure," said the man. "I was stealing wheelbarrows!"

IRATE WOMAN CUSTOMER: "I sent my little boy to your store this morning to buy two pounds of cookies. When he brought them home and I weighed them, I found there was only one pound. I suggest that you have your scales checked!"

BAKERY OWNER: "Madam, I suggest that you weigh your little boy!"

Bachelor Bob decided that it was time for him to marry and settle down. At the time he was going out with two girls whom he liked. One was a gorgeous girl, but not very bright, and the other was a rather homely opera singer. After many months of deliberation, Bob decided that brains and culture were more important than good looks, and so he married the opera singer.

No sooner was he married than he began to regret his choice. As a matter of fact, as the couple was driving away from the church, the bride found her new husband looking at her unpleasantly.

"What's the matter, darling?" she asked.

"For heaven's sake," replied Bob, "*sing* something!"

The summer resident came into the general store and looked around. It was quite a nice store, and there was a good selection of merchandise, but he was puzzled by the fact that half of the shelves were filled with boxes of soap of a particular brand.

"Hi!" he said to the storekeeper. "Nice store you have here."

"Thank you," said the storekeeper.

"From the looks of things, though, you must sell an awful lot of soap," added the summer resident.

"Nope," said the storekeeper. "I don't sell much soap at all. Hardly a case a year."

"Then why," asked the summer resident, "are your shelves piled so high with soap?"

"Well," drawled the storekeeper, "the feller I buy soap from — boy! Does he sell soap!"

A coyote was slinking around near the henhouse on a farm, trying to capture a nice fat chicken for dinner, but he wasn't able to break in. He was just about to leave when he noticed that the kitchen door of the farmhouse was open. Entering, he was overjoyed to behold a nice big five-pound baloney that the farmer's wife had left out on the kitchen table.

Greedily, the coyote ate all of the baloney. Then he felt so full and so good that he raised his head and yowled.

The farmer was upstairs, but when he heard the yowl, he grabbed his gun and ran downstairs and shot the coyote.

The moral of this story is simply this: When you're full of baloney, keep your mouth shut!

A wife kept very strict account of her husband's finances. She would take all of his salary each week, and then give him just enough money for lunch, carfare and cigarettes.

One day the husband came running home shouting, "Darling, you'll never guess what happened! I won a hundred thousand dollars in the Irish Hospital Sweepstakes!"

"And where," asked the wife, "did you get the money to buy a ticket?"

Mrs. Lish and Mrs. Tish were both out in their back yards hanging up the wash. Mrs. Lish walked over to the fence and said to Mrs. Tish:

"Have you heard that my son Jim is coming home next week?"

"Why, no," answered Mrs. Tish. "I thought that the Judge sentenced him to fifteen years in prison."

"He did," said Mrs. Lish. "But the parole board gave him seven years off for good behavior."

"Now, don't you feel *proud*," said Mrs. Tish, "having such a good son?"

First Catty Female: "My dear, what magnificent pearls those are! I can hardly believe they're real."

Second Catty Female: "Oh, they're real, all right, and I shudder when I think of how much money my husband must have spent on them."

First Catty Female: "Well, I just hope that he isn't trying to fool you. You know, you can always tell the real thing by biting them. Would you let me test them?"

Second Catty Female: "Of course, my dear, but I hope you remember that you can't test pearls with false teeth."

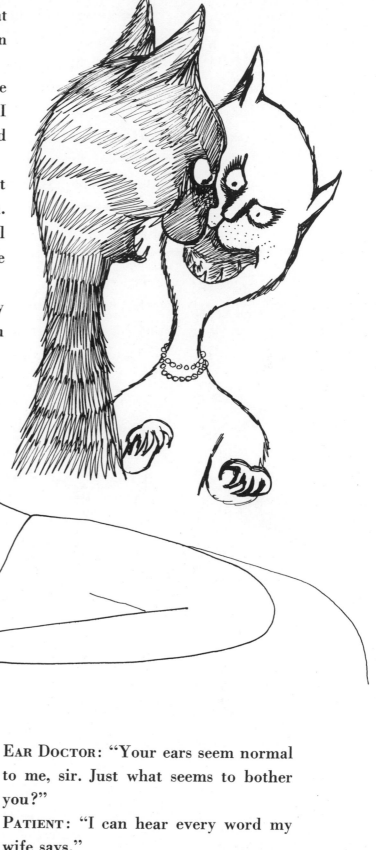

Ear Doctor: "Your ears seem normal to me, sir. Just what seems to bother you?"

Patient: "I can hear every word my wife says."

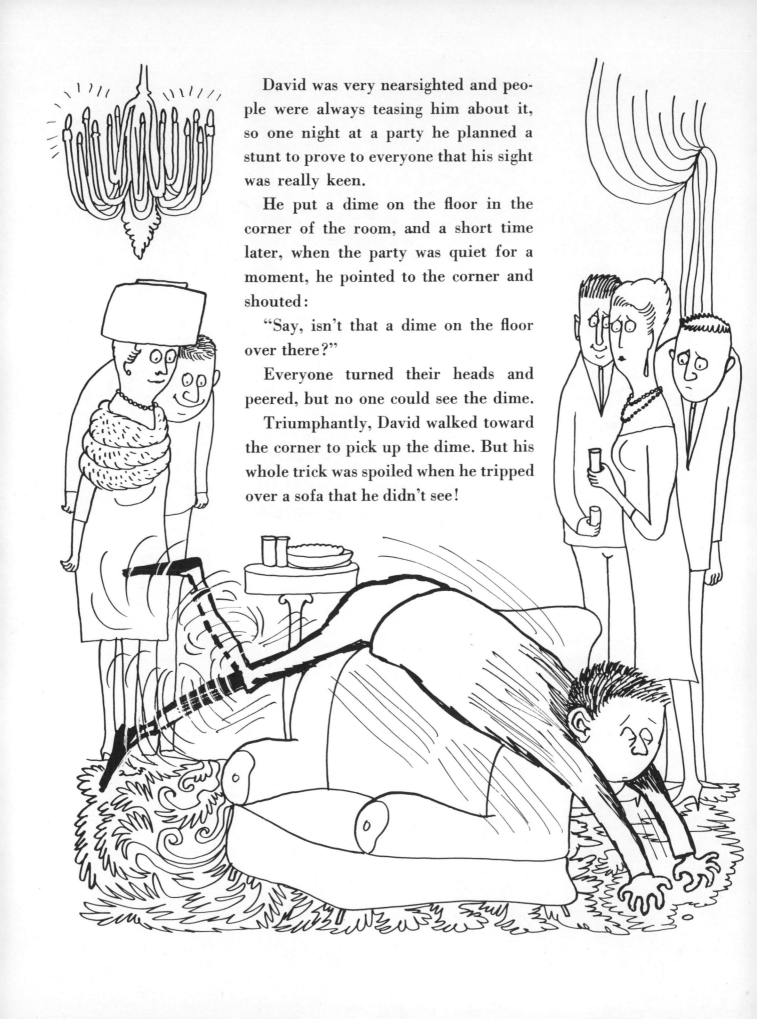

David was very nearsighted and people were always teasing him about it, so one night at a party he planned a stunt to prove to everyone that his sight was really keen.

He put a dime on the floor in the corner of the room, and a short time later, when the party was quiet for a moment, he pointed to the corner and shouted:

"Say, isn't that a dime on the floor over there?"

Everyone turned their heads and peered, but no one could see the dime.

Triumphantly, David walked toward the corner to pick up the dime. But his whole trick was spoiled when he tripped over a sofa that he didn't see!

A grizzly bear lumbered into a soda fountain, sat down on a stool, and ordered a chocolate soda. After he had finished the soda, he threw a five-dollar bill on the counter. The counterman took the bill, put it in the cash register and gave the grizzly bear four dollars change.

"Is that all the change I get?" asked the bear.

"Yes, sir," said the counterman. "Chocolate sodas are a dollar each here. And may I add that it has been a pleasure serving you. You are the first bear we have ever had as a customer."

"And probably the last," grumbled the bear. "At those prices!"

There was a little girl named Myrtle, who had a pet turtle that she loved very much.

One day, Myrtle's father came home and found Myrtle crying.

"Why are you crying, Myrtle?" he asked.

"Boo-hoo, my turtle died," sobbed Myrtle.

"Don't cry, Myrtle," said her father, trying to cheer her up. "We will get a cigar box to bury him in, and some flowers, and at least we can give him the nicest funeral a turtle ever had. You can even invite your friends."

Myrtle cheered up immediately, and

they got a cigar box and flowers, and invited her friends over for the funeral. They all made a solemn procession into the back yard, and Myrtle's father dug a hole for the grave. Then they all stood around and sang a sad and lovely song.

It was a beautiful funeral.

Just as they were about to close the cover on the cigar box and place it in the grave, the turtle poked his head out of his shell.

"Look, Myrtle, look!" cried Myrtle's father. "Your turtle is still alive!"

Myrtle looked at the turtle weaving his head. She looked at her friends. She looked at the flowers and the grave.

Then she looked at her father.

"Let's kill him!" she said.

A mother was complaining to her friend that her two sons were constantly squabbling over the division of things around the house.

"I just don't know what to do," she sighed.

"Oh, it's very simple to handle that," said her friend. "Just appoint one of them to always do the dividing — and allow the other one first choice!"

On the first day of school, the teacher was calling the roll. When she got to the letter S, she hesitated a minute.

"Shakespeare," she called.

"Here, teacher," said a little boy in the back row.

"What's your first name, Shakespeare?" asked the teacher.

"William, ma'am," answered the boy.

"That's a rather well-known name, isn't it?" asked the teacher.

"It should be!" said the boy. "I've lived in this neighborhood for more than ten years!"

The town drunkard was walking down Main Street one day, and he was amazed when the minister approached him and warmly shook his hand.

"John," said the minister, "I am very happy to know that you have turned over a new leaf. You don't know how overjoyed I was to see you at the prayer meeting last night."

"Oh," said the drunkard, "so *that's* where I was!"

Mr. Smith was proudly strolling through the park with his Great Dane on a leash, when he passed Mr. Dale who had a little yellow dog on a leash.

"You'd better keep that little yellow dog away from my Great Dane," said Mr. Smith. "He might just gobble him up in one bite."

Just then the Great Dane lunged at the little yellow dog. The little yellow dog just opened his jaws and snapped.

With a yelp and a howl, the Great Dane dragged the leash out of Mr. Smith's grasp and ran away with his tail between his legs.

"Say, what kind of dog do you call that?" asked Mr. Smith. "He frightened my Great Dane out of his wits."

"Well," drawled Mr. Dale, "before I painted him yellow, I called him an alligator."

The customer came into the bakery and spoke to the clerk:

"I would like to order a cake baked in the shape of a turtle, with a pink icing shell, green head and legs, and purple eyes."

"That will be a very difficult order," said the clerk, "and it will cost twenty-five dollars."

"Perfectly all right," said the customer. "I will pick it up next Thursday."

The following Thursday the customer came into the store.

"Is my cake ready?" he asked.

With a flourish, the clerk carried in this triumph of the baker's art. There it was! A gorgeous cake in the shape of a turtle, with pink icing shell, green head and legs, and purple eyes!

"Shall I pack it for you now?" asked the clerk with pride in his voice.

"You needn't bother," said the customer. "I'll eat it here."

FUZZY WUZZY WAS A BEAR.
FUZZY WUZZY HAD NO HAIR.
FUZZY WUZZY WASN'T FUZZY,
WAS HE?

MR. CRAIG: "My wife is just *too* neat and fussy about the house! Why, last night, at two A.M., I went to the kitchen to get a glass of milk, and when I came back, the bed was made!"

A dentist married a manicurist, and they've been fighting tooth and nail ever since.

Miss Dingle, the office secretary, came strolling in a little after ten o'clock.

"You should have been here at nine o'clock," said her boss.

"Really?" she asked. "What happened?"

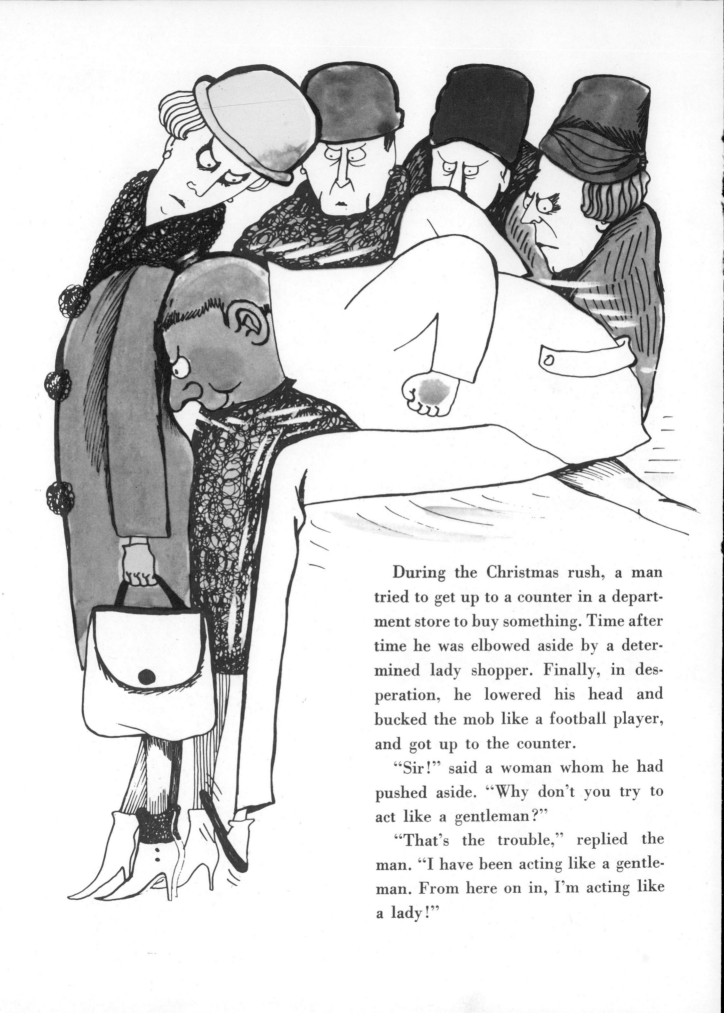

During the Christmas rush, a man tried to get up to a counter in a department store to buy something. Time after time he was elbowed aside by a determined lady shopper. Finally, in desperation, he lowered his head and bucked the mob like a football player, and got up to the counter.

"Sir!" said a woman whom he had pushed aside. "Why don't you try to act like a gentleman?"

"That's the trouble," replied the man. "I have been acting like a gentleman. From here on in, I'm acting like a lady!"

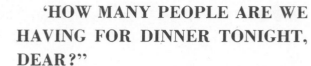

'HOW MANY PEOPLE ARE WE HAVING FOR DINNER TONIGHT, DEAR?''

— asked the cannibal.

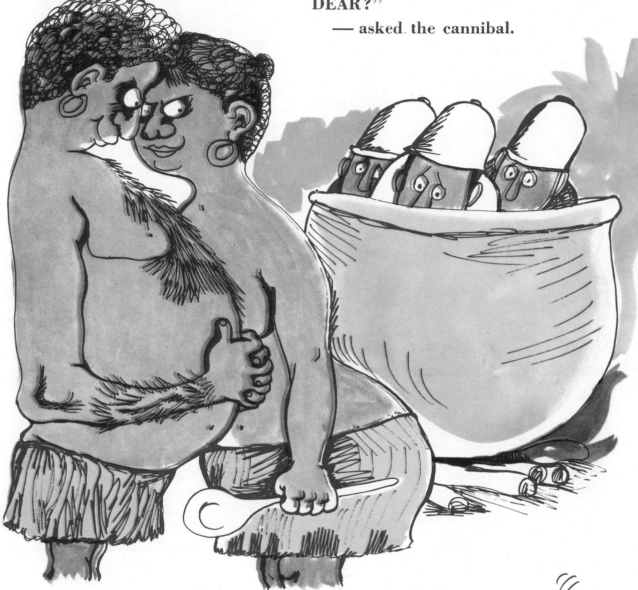

A baby sardine was frightened by an atomic submarine. She swam crying to her mother, who tried to comfort her.

"There, there!" she said. "Don't be frightened! It's only a can of people!"

There once was a little old man who sold shoelaces in front of the Stock Exchange Building. Among his steady customers was a stockbroker who drove up each day in a Rolls-Royce limousine. The first thing the stockbroker would do upon alighting from his car was to throw a dime in the old man's box.

This went on, day in and day out, for several years. Each morning the stockbroker would throw his dime in the old man's box, but he would never take a pair of shoelaces out of the box.

One day, just as the stockbroker was about to put his dime in the box, the old man addressed him:

"Excuse me, sir," said the old man, "but there is something I would like to tell you."

"I know, I know," said the stockbroker. "You want to know why I always throw a dime in the box and never take a pair of shoelaces."

"Oh, no, sir," replied the little old man. "I just want to inform you that the price of shoelaces has gone up to fifteen cents!"